Your Towns and Cities in the

Wirral

in the Great War

Dedicated to my daughter Stephanie

Also by Stephen McGreal and published by
Pen & Sword Books Ltd

The Cheshire Bantams.
The Zeebrugge and Ostend Raid
(Battleground Europe series).
Boesinghe (Battleground Europe series).
The War on the Hospital Ships 1914-1918.
Liverpool at War 1914-18.

Your Towns and Cities in the Great War

Wirral
in the Great War

Stephen McGreal

Pen & Sword
MILITARY

First published in Great Britain in 2014 by
PEN & SWORD MILITARY
An imprint of
Pen & Sword Books Ltd
47 Church Street
Barnsley
South Yorkshire S70 2AS

ISBN 978 1 78303 293 8

A CIP catalogue record for this book is available from the British Library.

Printed and bound in England by
CPI Group (UK) Ltd, Croydon, CR0 4YY

Pen & Sword Books Ltd incorporates the imprints of Aviation, Atlas,
Family History, Fiction, Maritime, Military, Discovery, Politics, History,
Archaeology, Select, Wharncliffe Local History, Wharncliffe True Crime,
Military Classics, Wharncliffe Transport, Leo Cooper, The Praetorian Press,
Remember When, Seaforth Publishing and Frontline Publishing.

For a complete list of Pen & Sword titles please contact
PEN & SWORD BOOKS LIMITED
47 Church Street, Barnsley, South Yorkshire, S70 2AS, England
E-mail: enquiries@pen-and-sword.co.uk
Website: www.pen-and-sword.co.uk

Contents

Acknowledgements

To faithfully encompass the conditions prevailing upon the home front, the author has extensively consulted contemporary (and government censored) local newspapers. The author wishes to thank the following people for their assistance in producing this work:

My long suffering friend Roni Wilkinson of Pen & Sword for his faith in my deliverance of a worthy addition to the Town & Cities series, and of course his customary patience and good humour as he turns another sow's ear into a silk purse.

Irene Moore for editing this work.

Fellow author Ian Boumphrey for kindly providing several scarce images from his outstanding collection of local postcards.

Peter Blackmore for sharing his Wallasey Town Hall hospital images.

The staff at Wirral Archives service, where I spent long hours scouring original editions of the Birkenhead newspapers.

Staff at Earlsden Road Reference Library for making available to this project the original editions of the *Wallasey News*.

The staff at Borough Road Reference Library for their interest in the project and allowing the reproduction of images from the Harding, Rathore albums. All other images are from the author's postcard collection and archive.

Introduction

The focus of commemoration during the centenary years of the First World War, will inevitably concentrate on the war of attrition and the appalling cost in human life suffered by all belligerents. The casualty figures will understandably highlight the consequences of the war of attrition, and perhaps omit any reference to the civilians killed on the home front due to enemy action. From 1914, defenceless women and children endured for the first time the horror of air raids, naval bombardments, black outs and food rationing. Dining tables across the land soon had vacant seats when men responded to Kitchener's call to arms or compulsory military service; many failed to return or came home broken in body or mind. In France, Britain's small professional army faced a David and Goliath battle but lacked the deadly slingshot to smite the most powerful military machine in the world – Germany.

An unprecedented arms race ensued, as all nations strove to deliver the tools and manpower so desperately needed in the front line. In doing so, the home front responded magnificently to the call 'Feed the Guns', the British war effort would involve, in one form or other, almost every inhabitant over school age. In 1798, income tax was implemented in Britain, to fund weapons and equipment for the Napoleonic wars, but taxation alone was inadequate to finance a twentieth century mechanised war. Every normal civilian activity became a means of fund raising, each day was equivalent to Red Nose Day, Children In Need Day and every other worthy cause rolled into one. The Great War was greatly financed by people, who asked for and received nothing what so ever from the state, but were still inspired by patriotism and allegiance to the king and the belief in their cause. This work, a long overdue ambition, explains how Wirral produced the all important sinews of war.

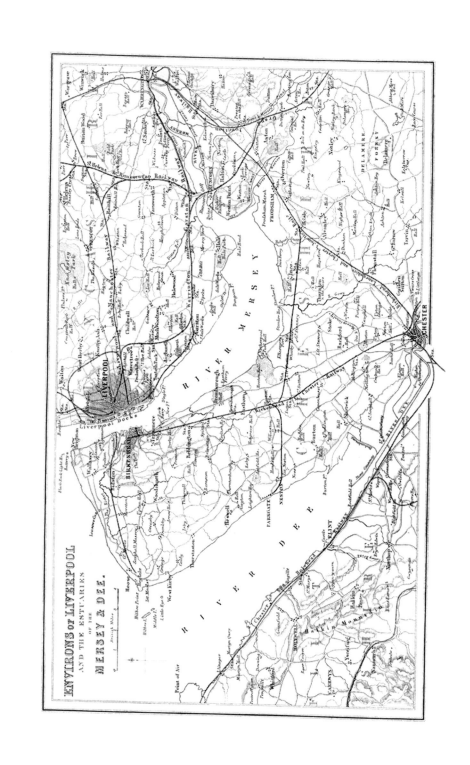

ENVIRONS OF LIVERPOOL
AND THE ESTUARIES
OF THE
MERSEY & DEE.

CHAPTER 1

A Summary of Nineteenth Century Wirral

In the North West of England lies the Wirral peninsula, originally the northern extremity of Cheshire until 1972 when political boundary changes resulted in the northern part becoming part of Merseyside. Wirral is approximately fifteen miles long by seven wide and almost surrounded by water, for it is bounded on the west by the River Dee and to the east by the River Mersey; the tidal estuaries of both rivers flow northwards and merge into the Irish Sea. The two principal Wirral towns are Birkenhead and Wallasey separated by a watery expanse of now almost redundant docklands, currently scheduled for a spectacular £4.5 billion re-development.

Along the more industrialised coast of Wirral flows the once bustling River Mersey, whose banks and quays appeared to offer employment in one form or other to most Merseyside families. On the Cheshire bank of the river, the first docks were opened in 1847 around the Wallasey Pool, through which ran an imaginary demarcation line separating both townships. The development of Birkenhead docks required the construction of a wall across the mouth of the pool and the damming up of the water behind it created the Great Float, around which quays and warehouses slowly developed. The new venture heralded a period of rivalry on both banks of the Mersey until 1855, when Liverpool Corporation purchased the rights of the Birkenhead Dock Trustees, bringing the control of Liverpool and Birkenhead docks under one

Wallasey Town Hall

authority. It was a shrewd move to ensure the Wirral docklands could never threaten the prosperity of the port of Liverpool by undercutting their high port fees.

The availability of deep water berths at the Great Float led to the construction circa 1895 of vast flour mills on the quayside, where vessels discharged their cargoes of flour and cereal products directly into Vernon, Rank and Spiller mills. The Wallasey ratepayers had witnessed great improvements in water supply, sanitation, education, a Wallasey police force and investment in the rail and highways infrastructure, but it was not until 1910 that the town achieved borough status, the first to be granted by George V. County borough status was granted on 1 April 1913.

According to the 1911 census, Wallasey Borough had 78,504 residents, many of whom would have witnessed, on 25 March 1914, George V and Queen Mary participate in the laying of the foundation stone for the new Wallasey Town Hall. However, due to world events the premises were not officially opened for their intended use until 3 November 1920.

Wirral's other principal town, Birkenhead was little more than a village until the beginning of the nineteenth century; by 1820 the population was a mere 200, compared to the Deeside villages of Neston and Parkgate with over 1,300 residents. In the same year the introduction of a reliable cross- river journey by steam ferry boat prompted Liverpool businessmen to establish grand homes in Birkenhead and commute to Liverpool. The Greenock businessman William Laird visited Liverpool looking for business opportunities; instead he recognised the potential of undeveloped Birkenhead. In 1824 Laird purchased a large tract of land on the edge of Wallasey Pool, where he established a boiler making works, rapidly followed by a shipbuilding yard. He envisaged converting the tidal pool into a great wet basin and docks linked to the River Dee by a proposed canal. The monopolising Liverpool Corporation thwarted the development by acquiring land on the south side of Wallasey Pool, but the land stood vacant for two decades until it was sold off in small lots. Amongst the purchasers were William Jackson and William Laird's eldest son, John, who formed a consortium and promoted a Parliamentary bill for the building of a great floating harbour minus the canal; the foundation-stone of the docks was laid in 1844 but the project's finances suffered one setback after another.

In 1847 the first two docks and associated warehouses opened, but

Birkenhead Docks

A PORTION OF THE MERSEY DOCK ESTATE AT BIRKENHEAD.

the scheme was in financial crisis and all construction work ended abruptly prompting an exodus of workers. Birkenhead Docks were in a state of insolvency when in 1855 an Act of Parliament transferred the ownership of the unfinished docks to Liverpool Corporation; three years later the newly constituted Mersey Docks and Harbour Board took control.

Despite the downturn the Improvement Commissioners of Birkenhead (including John Laird and William Jackson) pressed on with community improvements, including the first public park created at public expense. They improved the water supply, sewers were laid and roads were paved and the improvements attracted more businesses and workers. In 1857 Lairds moved to south of Woodside Ferry, Birkenhead. The yard had five graving docks and four building slipways which obliterated the last vestiges of the headland of birch trees or 'birken-head'. Four years later, having handed his business to his sons, John Laird retired from shipbuilding and was returned as the first Member of Parliament of the recently appointed Borough of Birkenhead, population 35,923. He was re-elected in three subsequent General Elections, the town prospered due to the success of the shipyard and his endeavour and he is justifiably described as 'the father of Birkenhead'.

The Great Western Railway Company (GWR) inaugurated in 1854 their London Paddington to Birkenhead express service, terminating initially at Monks Ferry, but extended in 1878 to Woodside station adjacent to the ferry. A local rail network followed linking most Wirral villages and expanding dock system with Chester and further afield. In 1886 the completion of the Mersey Railway Tunnel connected Cheshire and Lancashire; the line was electrified in 1903. The Town Hall opened in 1887, completing a square of fine Georgian terrace houses. The town's prosperity attracted Warrington businessman William Hesketh Lever whose factory produced 450 tons of 'Sunlight' soap a week. In 1888 Lever purchased sufficient land to build an extensive factory and, uniquely for the period, a village where his employees could live in a benign environment close to their work.

Another significant development occurred in 1903 when Laird Brothers amalgamated with the Sheffield steel company Charles Cammell and Co, manufacturers of steel castings and armour plate for warships. The merged company became Cammell Laird and Co who then expanded to 100 acres and created a further two graving docks. By the time of the 1911 census, Birkenhead had 130,794 inhabitants and their future looked rosy, for Great Britain was at the height of her economic and colonial power.

To most citizens it would have been incomprehensible to consider that the 28 June 1914 assassination of the Archduke Franz Ferdinand and his wife in Sarajevo, the capital of Bosnia, would precipitate a chain of events culminating in the outbreak of the Great War, now generally known as the First World War. The road to Armageddon was merely precipitated by the murder, for the root causes of the conflict are diverse, the primary causes being nationalistic ambitions, insecurity, expansion of territory and military brinkmanship.

Seeking reparations for the murders by Bosnian-Serb assassins, Austria-Hungary prompted by Germany made a series of uncompromising demands on Serbia who agreed to most of the demands, except for the issue of sovereignty. The British proposed a conference to arbitrate the issues; this was declined by Austria-Hungary and as a result, on 28 July 1914, war was declared on Serbia. Against such an incursion, the European powers were linked by international treaties of support so the next day Russia commenced mobilising troops to come to the aid of her Serbian ally. Russia refused German demands to demobilise troops, this led to the 1 August declaration of war; two days later Germany declared war on France.

Long-standing German preparations for war, required the army to rapidly advance in a great sweeping arc through France, in doing so Paris would fall, prompting the capitulation of France. To do so, Germany required free passage of its troops through neutral Belgium. The German march to victory was intended to be accomplished before Russia could fully deploy her troops, thus preventing an unsustainable war on two fronts.

On 3 August 1914, plucky Belgium refused German demands of egress across their nation, the following day Germany entered Belgium. It was a calculated gamble for Germany doubted Britain would honour their treaty to protect Belgium neutrality, especially as the British royal family were of German extraction. But, on 4 August Britain declared war in compliance with what the Germans scathingly called 'a scrap

If I could plant a tiny plug of lead in the region of your ———

FRANCE BOUNDARY

Shots to the rear

of paper'. A war that many had thought probable came to fruition from 11pm (midnight German time).

To prevent a run on the financial institutions, the bank holiday was extended for several days, but it only applied to banks. This gave banks and financial institutions time to ascertain how they stood, and to give the Government time to prepare and issue one pound and ten shilling notes in order that the banks should be able to meet demands on them for smaller currency than five pound notes. The new notes, which were payable in gold at the bank, were ready to the extent of £3,000,000 on 7 August, when the banks re-opened. Subsequent issues of notes at the rate of £5,000,000 a day relieved the pressure on London. On 10 August, over £2,600,000 of United States gold was received in London; the problem of providing currency was successfully met by the issue of the new notes.

A souvenir badge marking the declaration of war and the introduction of one pound notes

CHAPTER 2

1914 – Eager for a Fight

The prospect of war was disconcerting to the British who envisaged, if anything, a brief campaign in Europe culminating in the inevitable British victory. However, all was not well in old Albion, for industrial relations were in turmoil. On the Mersey August heralded in the fourth week of a struggle between dock bosses and their men for the right of recognition of trade unionism. In the meantime the approaching Bank Holiday offered other workers an opportunity to relax. In the summer months some three million Liverpool visitors took one of the seven

Pier and Ferry

New Brighton. The Landing Stage.

*Ham and Egg Parade and
New Brighton Tower*

ferry crossings or cheap excursion trains to the Wirral seaside resorts
of Hoylake, West Kirby and New Brighton.

New Brighton had a tower 100 feet taller than Blackpool; the Tower
Theatre seated 3,000 spectators and had the largest ballroom in the
north-west of England. A thirty-five acre pleasure ground surrounded
the base of the tower.

Amongst the theatres, The Tivoli Theatre offered a vocal and
orchestral concert featuring Louis Baxter's Casino Orchestra,
passengers arriving at the pier and pavilion might see Sydney James
and his famous strollers. Amongst the day-trippers on the ferry pier,
ladies of the 350-strong Wirral Women's Suffrage Society sold copies
of the *Common Cause*, their open-air meetings on New Brighton sands
were 'singularly successful'. On the outbreak of war the WSPU
suspended all hostilities and activities following the release of their

political prisoners, Germanic activities later ensured female emancipation would make undreamed of progress.

Across the resort sands at the mouth of the Mersey stands the Fort Perch Rock Battery (now an aviation archaeology and maritime museum) built of Runcorn sandstone. Originally commissioned for the protection of Liverpool during the Napoleonic Wars, by the time the government had finally agreed on the design Napoleon had died. Completed in April 1829, and continually modified, the original guns were replaced in 1910 by three superior Mark VII 6-inch guns. As the storm clouds of war gathered the 120-strong garrison of the Lancashire and Cheshire Royal Garrison Artillery (RGA) commanded by Major C.J. Luya took delivery of a large consignment of ammunition. The companies were about to depart to Shoeburyness for their annual camp, but received orders to hold in readiness for mobilization. The battery also received orders that no vessel was allowed to pass without being examined and constant communication was kept with other coast defence stations. The public were warned not to enter within a circumscribed area of the battery, especially after dark, for the sentries had orders to shoot any person discovered nearby.

Overnight the nation began to metamorphose into a military garrison, significant docks and quays became defended ports, regulations stated:

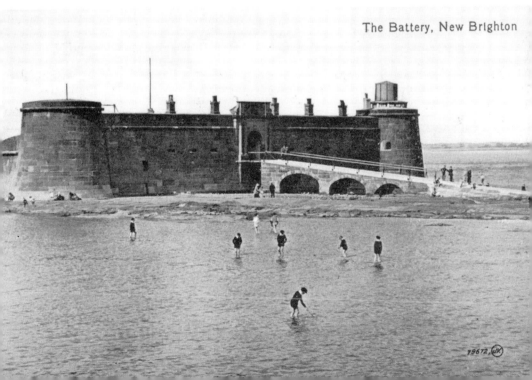

The Battery, New Brighton

Boats have to pass through the examination anchorage and be examined by the examining officer. No vessel must be navigated or be at anchor between sunrise and sunset seaward of the line joining the Seaforth battery and New Brighton pier except she be entering or leaving port.

Several hours after the declaration of war, at 7am a large Norwegian sailing vessel failed to respond to the heave-to signal from the New Brighton battery. On command the battery fired the first British shot of the war, but the elevation was too high, the shell hurtled past the vessel's bow and landed on the opposite bank; a second shell hit the bow of an anchored Allen liner. After the authorities boarded the Norwegian schooner, the arrested captain declared that 'he was unaware the war had begun'.

The following day *The Birkenhead News* reported:

'The hand of war is already tightening its brutal grip upon the throat of industry. Orders for the mobilisation of the whole of His Majesty's Auxiliary Forces were issued yesterday, with the exception of the National Reserve, with the result that the staff of nearly every business and industrial concern in the town will to a more or less degree shortly be affected. As an indication of this, it might be mentioned that at Messrs Lever Bros works at Port Sunlight there are employed about 200 Army and Naval Reservists and several hundred Territorials and National Reservists. The number of citizen soldiers at Cammell Laird and Co is even greater than that at Port Sunlight, while a complete company of Naval Reserves is raised entirely in these yards.'

The first week in August was a statutory holiday for Cammell Laird workers, but the declaration of war endangered the Royal Navy and the mercantile marine, shipyard officials were despatched to holiday resorts with instructions for the men to return to work. Among the vessels under construction were three cruisers and one flotilla leader, these were delivered to the Admiralty months before their contracted delivery date. (HMS *Caroline*, one of the three remaining First World War British warships, recently received a substantial tourism grant).

At the end of 1913, the neighbouring ship repairers, Clover, Clayton and Co Ltd, received a contract to manufacture several thousand horse

Clovers Dry Docks

stall kits, which were stored in the yard for emergencies. Immediately hostilities commenced a large number of these were distributed around the coast to various ship repair firms for fitting out transports.

During the bank holiday weekend, the local territorial battalion of part time soldiers, the 4th Cheshire Regiment (4/Cheshire) had some fifty men in camp near Eastham lock. But alerted to the probable need to mobilise they returned to their main drill hall in Grange Road West where 'a large crowd of men were clamouring to enlist'.

The *History of the Cheshire Regiment* recalls:

> '*The mobilization scheme provided for the local purchase of clothing, equipment and transport. Two officers were sent out early in the morning with requisitions, and they did their job without a hitch, thus forestalling the Royal Engineers and Yeomanry who were doing the same thing. The transport was a queer sight. Every sort and condition of cart was requisitioned, including street watering carts; the horses varied from hunters to heavy draft horses and the harness was all of civilian pattern and in various states of repair. A piece of waste land near the drill hall became the transport lines.*'

4 Cheshire Drill Hall

The battalion was known locally as 'The Greys', a legacy of the days when they were attired in grey uniform. The first wartime edition of *The Birkenhead and Cheshire Advertiser* reported:

> *'The Deeside Greys' company have been quartered in the church schools, Heswall since the outbreak of war ready to proceed at a moment's notice to whatever station they are attached. The company, which is comprised of West Kirby, Heswall and Neston men, is under the command of Captain W.J. Newton, during the interval have gone through a course of firing at targets on Heswall beach...'*

The severity of the situation became evident when Captain and Adjutant H.E. Pateshall placed an official press notice demanding 4/Cheshire personnel report to their company headquarters in marching order with kit bags packed. Any failing to appear would be treated as a deserter. On completion of mobilisation, the battalion entrained on 9 and 10 August for Shrewsbury.

"BE PREPARED."

A few days after the outbreak of war a deputation of Birkenhead Scoutmasters met in the town hall and offered the services of some 800 Boy Scouts to the town's civil and defence authorities. The offer was warmly accepted and for many weeks the Mersey Railway absorbed a great part of the Scout troops. Every station on the system, from Liverpool Central to Green Lane and Park station, was served by scouts who were guarding cables and telegraphs from interference. The scouts also guarded various reservoir and pumping stations, the night work being carried out by the special constables.

Overnight, the army suddenly required thousands more draft horses for hauling supply wagons and artillery, also superior-bred equines for officers' mounts. The locality was swept for horses and vehicles for war, the corporation street cleaning department immediately lost seventeen horses, as did a diverse range of businesses. The disgruntled owners received a payment voucher from a quartermaster but the valuation was determined by the military. Prior to dispersal, the local horses commandeered for the Cheshire Field Company and Royal Engineers, based at Harrowby Road, were gathered at Tranmere Rovers football ground. The horses acquired for the Welsh Division of the

Horses and carts were requisitioned for the military.

Army Service Corps (ASC) were held at Bebington Showground (now The Oval); the livestock at both sites was kept under armed guard, including those in fields at Temple Road.

The irate owners were powerless, any prospect of having their property returned evaporated, for on 8 August, the House of Commons, passed in five minutes, emergency wartime regulations for the British government. The Defence of the Realm Act (DORA) granted the government powers to suppress published criticism, imprison without trial and to commandeer resources, including buildings or land required for the war effort; the act was regularly supplemented throughout the war.

Immediately following the start of hostilities an orchestrated wave of xenophobia swept the country; non-British citizens were now treated with suspicion. Residents were encouraged to assist the police and military authorities by keeping close observation on all foreigners (dubbed aliens), especially Germans and report any suspicious movements to the police.

Aliens required a police permit to live in Birkenhead and Wallasey and could not travel more than five miles from their residence without police permission. Permits were also required for possession of a motor car, motor cycle or aircraft. They were further prohibited from possessing firearms, ammunition or explosives, or more than three gallons of flammable liquid, any signalling apparatus, carrier or homing pigeons, and any cipher books or other means of secret correspondence.

The draconian treatment of long-standing members of the community arose from the increasing paranoia of enemy sympathisers embedded in the communities. It was feared the spies might supply military information to the enemy to facilitate invasion, provide targets for hostile airships, or sabotage the water supply or railways. To protect public property and to compensate for the depletion of the police force due to mobilisation of reservists, Birkenhead and other boroughs swiftly recruited volunteer special constables.

As the Mersey was one of the nation's defended ports, within days 3,000 troops arrived in Birkenhead alone

THE IDEA—
THOUGHT I WAS A BALLY ALIE

to protect the docks and shipyards. Four Special Reserve infantry battalions were assigned to Mersey Defences. The 3rd (Special Reserve) battalion of the Cheshire Regiment (3/Cheshire) was mobilized in August 1914, they assembled in Chester where the 500-strong force drew its war equipment and stores and proceeded to its war station in Birkenhead. From their headquarters in Gamlins Furniture Depot, the officers arranged the occupation of strategic Wirral locations, including an outpost on Hilbre Island, and guarding Birkenhead docks. The Cheshires' appearance in the docks inflamed an ongoing dock strike, but eventually commonsense prevailed.

The efficient transition to military garrison progressed with the arrival of the Royal Artillery, who took up a dominant position on Bidston Hill. The sandstone ridge with a peak of 231 feet (70m) is

Lever Brothers St Johns Ambulance Brigade bid farewell

covered with 100 acres of heath and woodland and overlooks the tip of Wirral. From this strategic position the artillery acted as a look-out station for the Mersey Dock and Harbour Board and threatened to endanger enemy vessels attempting to navigate the Rock Channel. Regular troops also moved into Leasowe lighthouse and the nearby castle had already been turned to military use. To prevent German 'tip and run' raiders the navigation lights at the entrance to the River Dee were extinguished.

Industrial relations of the time were poor, particularly in the Mersey docks where an abundance of workers seeking unskilled work allowed unscrupulous employers to take advantage; wartime inflation, particularly on staple foods, further aggravated the situation. Within a week Birkenhead bakers twice raised bread prices, lard and bacon rose by fifty per cent, sugar doubled in price, butter and tea increased significantly.

Throughout the conflagration, Lever Brothers made a significant contribution to the war effort, both in men and materiel, the company's earliest volunteers were the members of the firms St John Ambulance Brigade. They paraded before the chairman of the company and said 'goodbye' on the third morning of the war, followed soon after by other contingents. About this time Levers despatched fifty motor cars to the front.

Far from the front line were the Bidston Hill Territorials who were alerted to the presence of a man in a grey suit in the lower wood acting in a suspicious manner. Shortly after midnight on 10 August an armed guard was turned out, and they proceeded to beat the bushes, some of the men being in advance of the others. Seven or eight shots were fired and suddenly there was a scream and a cry of 'Oh, I've been shot'. The guard hurried forward and found Private Louis Morice lying suffering from a wound a few inches below his ribs, he died a few minutes later – he had been in the army for one week. It was possible either a comrade stumbled over a log and inadvertently fired his rifle or in the darkness the shadowy figure of Morice was mistaken for the spy.

The 20-year old soldier received a full military funeral at Ford Cemetery, Liverpool. An extensive enquiry held in the reading room of Bidston village by the West Cheshire Coroner returned an open verdict.

Most leaders asserted the war would be over by Christmas, but the recently appointed Secretary of War, Lord Kitchener, vehemently disagreed. On 8 August, he called for 100,000 volunteers between the age of 19 and 30 to join the British Army; the response was phenomenal. Within a fortnight, in a wave of patriotism, 100,000 men of all social classes enlisted to serve for the duration in a war they expected to be satisfactorily concluded by Christmas 1914.

In preparation for the waves of recruits, the War Office requisitioned countless commodious premises including the vacant Hooton Hall near Ellesmere Port where a racecourse provided revenue to offset the hall's overheads. The races had ended abruptly within a few days of the start of hostilities. The elegant sandstone mansion became a military hospital, a training camp and an officers' mess, the other ranks would have less salubrious billets.

On 28 August, Kitchener called for a further 100,000 men, the response eclipsed previous recruitment. A few days earlier, Lord Kitchener and Lord Derby discussed the latter's suggestion of a battalion of men raised from the commercial offices of Liverpool who would serve together as comrades, in the same manner as the 10/Royal Fusiliers, known unofficially as 'The Stockbrokers Battalion'. Kitchener sanctioned the concept of a battalion raised from men who worked and met socially. When Derby's 27 August call to arms appeared in the Liverpool press, recruits converged on the advertised venue, the 5/King's drill hall.

Lord Derby invited the assembled volunteers to report on the morning of Monday, 31 August to St George's Hall where the great business houses of Liverpool set up individual attestation tables. Such was the clamour to enlist, in just over one week Lord Derby had raised over 3,000 Merseyside recruits, sufficient for three battalions of Pals. They were initially known as the 1st City, 2nd City and 3rd City battalions or the 1st, 2nd and 3rd Pals. Later they were officially entitled the 17th, 18th, 19th Service battalions of the King's Liverpool Regiment. By

Lor! And here I've tried for thirty years, and can't get one!'

An enterprising postcard photographer captures for all time the 23 September 1914 arrival of the Liverpool comrades at Hooton Park.

The 2nd Pals at Hooton Park taken outside their stable billet. Number one and two companies were quartered in loose boxes, nine men to each box.

Wirral battalion recruits in Central Park, Wallasey on 1 September.

early November, a fourth battalion the 20th KLR came into being, surplus recruits formed two reserve Pals battalions.

Sourcing suitable accommodation for the recruits proved difficult. Men of the 1st City battalion were billeted at the empty watch factory in Prescot, the 2nd City crossed the river to Hooton Park in Wirral, the 3rd City lacked billets, requiring the men to overnight at home or seek lodgings near Sefton Park where they trained daily.

On 1 September at a Port Sunlight meeting the suggestion of a Wirral battalion of the Cheshire Regiment was warmly greeted. A local MP Gershom Stewart conducted a series of recruitment meetings, however at Wallasey, due to earlier recruitment, only 250 recruits came forward.

The post war *Birkenhead News Victory Souvenir* recalled:

'There was a rush on the part of Lever Brothers' office men to the Pals battalions in Liverpool, raised at the call of Lord Derby, and on the part of the works employees to the recruiting station opened in the Gladstone Hall for the Wirral battalion, in the raising of which Mr Gershom Stewart, MP, was especially interested. At that hall alone, as early as 1 September 500 men had been recruited and Mr Gershom Stewart thanked Port

Sunlight for what he called the 'magnificent response' that it was making to the country's call.'

To facilitate the enlistments the soap factory provided offices and clerks and medicals and attestations were swiftly completed. Within a few days Port Sunlight had mustered 700 volunteers for the fledgling Wirral Battalion who gathered in the Auditorium on Sunday, 6 September for a 'God Speed' service. The next morning excited crowds accompanied the recruits as they marched to the works railway halt where they departed for Chester.

All the clerks with one exception joined the Pals, the 'stay at home,' experienced humiliation. One morning he became the recipient of a number of petticoats, blouses etc, the press reported it was understood he had not yet made use of his numerous presents!

Also, on the eve of their departure the 311 strong Wallasey Comrades, now supplemented by agricultural workers from outlying villages, attended divine service at St Hilary's church. Next morning, they boarded a special train at Seacombe station for Chester where they joined the 700 other Wirral battalion recruits.

After alighting at Chester, Sir William Lever proudly led the battalion to Chester Castle where they were put under the command of

Families seeing soldiers off from Port Sunlight village

The third contingent of Wirral battalion recruits departing from Seacombe

Captain Field. The Wirral comrades initially went to Tidworth where they commenced a year of training. The battalion should have been designated the 9th (Service) Cheshire battalion but inexplicably, upon adoption by the War Office, the battalion became the 13th (Service) Cheshire battalion.

As they left, Birkenhead Borough Hospital continued arrangements to accommodate seventy wounded or ill servicemen in the hospital and a thirty-four bed annexe in Roy Laird's house, 25 Devonshire Place. The public donated £15,000 towards the decoration and conversion cost of the hospital annexe, it was unwittingly the beginning of some four years of fund raising for worthy causes. Within two years the Borough Hospital had three annexes, 25 Devonshire Place, Shrewsbury Road and James Street, the latter also had an annexe financed mainly by Palm Grove Wesleyan Church. As the war escalated wealthy benefactors loaned property to philanthropic organisations to aid the amelioration of military wounded. The trickle of fundraising would rapidly develop into an inundation of flag days and street collections; the beneficiaries would soon arrive.

The vanguard of the 100,000 strong British Expeditionary Force (BEF) reached France on 7 August. After a few weeks' concentration, the British II Corps advanced to the south-east corner of Belgium,

2 Park Road South was used as a Red Cross work depot.

congregating around the town of Mons where the Germans delivered a terrific onslaught. The Cheshire's regimental history for the period states, of twenty-five officers and 952 other ranks, only seven officers and 200 other ranks remained.

Over half the battalion were reservists who three weeks earlier had hastily rejoined the battalion; the BEF survivors were now in a headlong retreat towards the River Marne. It would take time for the wounded to filter back to the United Kingdom where few hospital administrators could have predicted the enormity of the task on which they were embarking.

Ahead of the game was the Birkenhead Red Cross Work Depot which opened on 8 August at 2 Park Road South, the first room being provided by the committee of the Jubilee Nurses' Institute. Larger premises at 68 Balls Road followed; later number 64 was acquired followed by a nearby house in Barnard Road. In these premises a weekly average of 400 voluntary lady workers produced garments, comforts and other requisites for sailors and soldiers.

The earlier press coverage of Kitchener successfully attracting his 100,000 volunteers had a negative effect on further recruitment. The indifference to the situation arose from the mistaken belief that further volunteers were not necessary. But there came sudden enlightenment,

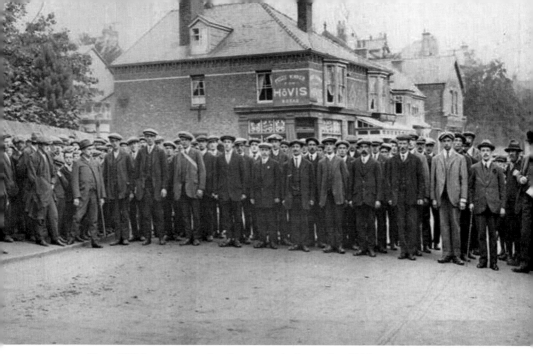

Heswall Volunteers pose for the camera in September 1914

which acted as a catalyst to recruitment in the censored press accounts of the retreat from Mons. Most people read through the lines and realised the gravity of the situation.

To aid the expansion of the army, each county was at first expected to raise one extra war service battalion to supplement the existing territorial battalions. The territorial units existed solely for home defence, the volunteers could not be ordered overseas. However, provisions in the form of an 'Imperial Service' section were made to enable a territorial to serve overseas if required. Those who made the declaration wore a rectangular white metal Imperial Service badge on their uniform jacket.

Wirral pre-war army infantry recruits generally opted to enlist into the Cheshire Regiment whose main depot was located at Chester Castle. Recruits wishing to serve with the Cheshires on a part-time basis joined one of the local companies of 'The Greys'.

Another long established unit, the Harrowby Road based Cheshire Field Company Royal Engineers, were recruited almost exclusively from Wirral men. In the early months of the war an Imperial Service section was embodied in addition to the home service unit. In early winter 1914, the overseas detachment was the first Territorial company of the Royal Engineers to be sent to the front.

1/4 Cheshire Territorials outside their billet, note the Imperial Service badges.

The Cheshire Brigade Company, Army Service Corps' supply and transport sections also served overseas.

Mention should also be made of the 1/10 battalion the King's Liverpool Regiment, arguably better known as the Liverpool Scottish. This rather elite territorial unit, comprising white-collar city types contained a strong element of New Brighton residents. On 13 August the battalion departed for Edinburgh to guard against a German invasion of the Firth of Forth.

Foreigners of a less belligerent nature now arrived on British shores, the displaced Belgian refugees often arrived in a pathetic condition,

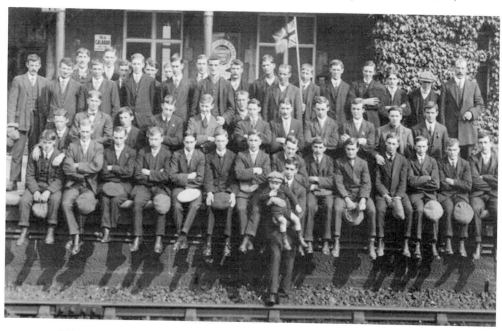

Willing recruits at Little Sutton station September 1914.

the clothes they stood in being their sole possessions. As their numbers increased, the tide of humanity was dispersed throughout the nation where benevolent organisations provided food and shelter. By mid-September, nine Belgian refugees were accommodated in a house at Parkgate Square, and ten Belgian soldiers with minor wounds were being treated at Parkgate Convalescence Home. Birkenhead

Come under the Banner that
never comes down.

Corporation made available a handsome old residence 'The Towers', situated in Victoria Park. The forty-three bed mansion opened for three days for public inspection during which Boy Scouts collected £48 for the Belgian Relief Fund.

On 3 October *The Wallasey News* reported:

> *'The first batch of Belgian refugees to arrive in Wallasey, composed of a mother and six children, arrived on 1 October and were taken to the Cenacle, Atherton Street, New Brighton where they received every attention from the Sisters of the Convent. The family were from Louvain and only spoke Flemish, the youngest child was five months old and the eldest fifteen. Mrs Cowhey had made arrangements to receive another batch at 23 Warwick Drive, Liscard.'*

According to *The Birkenhead Advertiser* the Hulme Hall refugees comprised forty-two men, thirty-two women and thirty-seven children with ages ranging from two and a half to 72. They remained there for five weeks as guests of Port Sunlight, the locals donated more than one hundred parcels of clothes and toys.

During the pre-war arms race the Royal Navy's Grand Fleet and

Hulme Hall Port Sunlight

HMS Hogue and two sister ships were torpedoed and sunk within minutes of each other.

Germany's High Seas Fleet underwent rapid expansion. The British warships may have outnumbered those of the German fleet but the Kaiser's vessels had superior design, weaponry and heavier armoured plates. As the summer of 1914 gave way to autumn the Royal Navy patrolled the North Sea to restrict the German High Seas Fleet, shield the east coast against invasion, operate a distant blockade of German ports and guard the North Sea exits. Within this watery expanse the world's two largest navies feinted and parried blows in minor skirmishes, neither side wishing to expose their 'castles of steel' to unnessary risk that may widen or lessen the balance of naval seapower. However this equilibrium was threatened by the success of German naval mines and the coming of age of the submarine.

On 22 September, three obsolete British cruisers *Aboukir, Hogue* and *Cressy* were patrolling in file off the Dutch coast unaware they were covertly observed from the German submarine *U9*. In rapid sucession Captain Lieutenant Otto Weddigen fired a series of torpedoes, his three targets quickly plunged to the seabed claiming

1,459 lives. The tragedy humiliated the Royal Navy, the submarine had come of age and altered forever naval tactics.

A few weeks later, 20 October marked another turning point in the war at sea when the coal carrying *Glitra* was intercepted by *U17* off the Norwegian coast. A boarding party scuttled the vessel, making her the first Great War merchantman sunk by a submarine.

Commercial photographers took thousands of images for picture postcards and had no shortage of subjects, who generally stared solemnly at the camera lens as evidenced by the stern ladies of St Bede's café, a popular venue for Cheshire Regiment men.

Throughout the conflict certain naval brigades would fight alongside

The café in St Bede's parish hall, Upton Road was opened on 22 September 1914

soldiers, in the trenches. With the situation in Flanders becoming increasingly desperate the First Lord of the Admiralty, Winston Churchill, convinced the cabinet to deploy three brigades of surplus naval troops at Antwerp, including the Royal Navy Volunteer Reserve, Mersey Division. Part of the Second Naval Brigade contained a considerable number of Cammell Laird men. The brigades arrived on 6 October, as the Belgian government was vacating the city, the next day the city was evacuated, the defenders retreated and Antwerp was entered by the Germans on 9/10 October.

Long before war broke out the West Lancashire Territorial Association had arranged with Liverpool Corporation that in the event of the mobilization of the Territorials, the Infectious Diseases Hospital at Fazakerley, Liverpool should be utilised as a military hospital. This was formally agreed on 5 August, and Lieutenant Colonel Burns Gemmel was immediately given permission to establish the 1st

Bravo! Territorials

There's none can say you lag,
In answering your Country's call
To rally round the Flag
Each one of you has proved himself
A Briton staunch and true,
Determined, that the whole wide world
Shall see what you can do.

Western General Hospital in the institution which, after being thoroughly disinfected, opened as a 520-bed military hospital. Local soldiers were the first patients until 22 September when the hospital ship *Eloby* brought the first casualties from France. On 1 October another influx of wounded were detrained from the first ambulance train to arrive at Aintree station. Shortly afterwards an inaugural batch of thirty patients was transferred to Birkenhead Borough Hospital.

The officer in charge of 1st Western was also responsible for all the military hospitals across a considerable area beyond Liverpool, excluding Red Cross and St John auxiliary hospitals. A successful appeal throughout the area for additional bed space brought an immediate response; each new district hospital became a satellite ward of the 1st Western General Hospital. As the war escalated 3,348 regional beds were made available or six times more than the original number at Fazakerley, this number excluded the auxiliary hospital beds.

Meanwhile further civilian restrictions were introduced, a 21

Arrowe Park Hall, through the generosity of Miss Dora Schuntz of Childwall Hall, served throughout the war as a fifty-bed military hospital.

October amendment to DORA banned fireworks and bonfires, both potential navigating beacons for any belligerent warships; the timely order also prevented Bonfire Night celebrations.

Pyrotechnics were in abundance in France and Flanders as both sides attempted to outflank each other, each abortive turning action taking the belligerents closer to the Belgian coast. The line of scattered defences, usually little more than shallow ditches, were gradually consolidated and connected by trenches. The Western Front, comprising a 400-mile network of trenches, soon extended from the Swiss border to the North Sea.

The war-displaced civilians continued to arrive on these shores, but on 28 October the local authorities refused to allow further aliens into the Wirral peninsula. This included Belgians and the

The dotted line is part of the Western Front

proposed provision of a West Kirby refugee house was blocked. As the government was suspicious of the allegiance of some aliens, a policy of internment commenced. At Douglas on the Isle of Man a camp originally used by the Territorial Army for annual camps was adapted to accept 5,000 male internees; women were not interned. A second and much larger timber hutment camp, regimentally laid out over 22 acres, was constructed at Knockaloe, near Peel. By the end of the war some 24,000 men were incarcerated there.

Meanwhile on the Western Front, the Belgian Army was fighting alongside the BEF in the First Battle of Ypres. On 19th October General Sir Douglas Haig's I Corps successfully counter-attacked and effectively ended the German drive towards Calais. By now the BEF had suffered unprecedented casualties, the troops were exhausted and grimly hanging on awaiting reinforcements. Lord Kitchener mistrusted the fighting ability of the Territorials who were primarily engaged in guarding ports, entrenching along the east coast or guarding railways. By necessity selected 'Imperial Service' Territorial battalions were now ordered to mobilise for overseas service.

The Liverpool Scottish, now at Tunbridge Wells, Kent departed on 1 November for Southampton, where they crossed the Channel on the SS *Maiden*. By 21 November 1914, five mounted Yeomanry regiments and twenty-one Territorial battalions were in France and Flanders.

But the flames of war now reached Asia, where Germany's successful courting of Turkey induced the ailing Ottoman Empire to align with Germany. Their United Kingdom residents were now classified as aliens and were legally required to obtain residence permits to live in the Mersey Defences prohibited area.

In Wallasey a new Voluntary Aid Detachment formed; ten of the twenty members were trained nurses, the remainder held first aid certificates. The executors of the late J.C. Stead allowed the use of his Penkett Road residence as a temporary forty-bed hospital. At the beginning of November the first twenty wounded patients were transferred from Fazakerley to Wallasey in motors loaned by the New Brighton Motor Coach Company. With one exception the men had received their front line wounds within the last ten days.

78 Penkett Road today, now two separate dwellings, the left part of 'Stoneycroft' a former Red Cross hospital, looks according to faded press images, as it did during the First World War. Conveniently located at 20 Penkett Road was the Wallasey branch of the War Dressings Association.

Dressing HQ today

In the interim, at Hooton Park, Wirral the 2nd Pals who became the 18th (Service) Battalion of the King's Liverpool Regiment, were undergoing rigorous training in the art of soldiering. After a 6am parade in running clothes a two-mile jog around the racecourse preceded a 7.30am breakfast. After a 9am parade companies marched off to drill which included physical drill, rifle drill with the rifles as used by the 'Terriers', and company and battalion drill. Daily trench digging and bi-weekly ten-mile route marches all built up the men's stamina, and built an appetite for the 5pm tea.

The Pals concept struck a chord with volunteers, leading to the

Hooton Park: raw recruits are in the foreground with more soldierly looking rifle-equipped men in the distance.

raising of a fourth Pals battalion which was completed in three days. On 27 November General Sir Henry McKinnon visited Hooton to inspect the comrades or Pals battalion. Six days later the second battalion relocated to recently completed billeting huts at Knowsley camp, where the four Pals battalions commenced training as an infantry brigade. The all-Merseyside 89 Brigade formed part of the 30th Division, the first of the Pals divisions.

In May 1917, the 18/King's Liverpool officers and men, erected a memorial tablet in Hooton parish church to commemorate the 'gracious ministry of healing discharged by many ladies of the district to the sick soldiers of the battalion', a VAD bed was also provided in Liverpool.

The War Office in mid September refused to authorise a Birkenhead Pals battalion, but a later incident in the recruiting office at 109a Grange Road led to the town raising two unique battalions of infantry. An aspiring recruit failed to comply with the minimum height requirement, indignant at yet another rejection, the man offered to fight anyone in the building before eventually being ejected. When Alfred Bigland MP heard of the incident he sought permission from Lord Kitchener to recruit men rejected on grounds of height, but otherwise fit. On 18 November *The Birkenhead News* published Bigland's letter advising of the raising of a battalion of men shorter than 5ft 3ins in height and recruiting commenced on 30 November.

Enlistments started on Monday and by Tuesday night a battalion (1,100 men) had been raised. On Wednesday the flow of recruits from throughout the kingdom continued. On Thursday morning Alfred Bigland received War Office permission to raise a second battalion – he already had 600 men. By Thursday night 2,200 'short but wide' men had enrolled, within four days two Bantam battalions were raised.

The first battalion was billeted at Mersey Park School until the adaptation of the Bebington agricultural showground (now the Oval Sports Centre) was completed. The second battalion was accommodated mainly in the Infants Department of Rock Ferry Council School, Ionic Street or billeted in the community.

The First and Second Bigland's Birkenhead Bantams, when adopted by the War Office, became the 15th (Service) and 16th (Service) battalions of the Cheshire Regiment.

Another fine band of volunteers were the Voluntary Aid

Detachments (VAD) raised in 1909, with the assistance of the Red Cross and the Order of St John to provide medical services in time of war. The outbreak of war found the Women's VAD well established in Birkenhead, but there was no men's detachment to undertake the conveyance of the wounded to the various hospitals. Fortunately there was a small branch of St John's Ambulance Brigade anxious to do their bit by receiving the hospital trains terminating at Woodside Station. The willing volunteers evolved into the VAD Cheshire 19 (A and B) and the Cheshire Transport, 19T commanded by Roland Jackson, Chief Transport Officer. The 130 male VAD workers were all drawn from the railways, shipbuilding and repair yards.

In late September the Convalescent Home at Parkgate, after being re-decorated, opened for the reception of ten bad surgical cases and thirty convalescent servicemen. During the opening ceremony twenty uniformed members of the Neston Red Cross Society mingled with

The chalked twenty-three on the right-hand door frame indicates twenty-three soldiers housed within, evidently Bantams were billeted inside the Fairfield public house.

Members of the Birkenhead VAD

guests. After tea an exhibition of drill was given by the thirty strong local ambulance corps who possessed six stretchers! During the proceedings Mr Thompson on behalf of the Royal Infirmary Chester, thanked the Hon Mrs H.N. Gladstone for funding the expensive refitting costs.

After the 1 November formation of the first VAD to be formed in Wallasey, the Red Cross Men's VAD (Cheshire No 15) also participated in the reception and dispersal of wounded.

As Christmas approached, the guardians of the Tranmere Union Infirmary (a former workhouse, later St Catherine's Hospital) offered the almost new H Block for the reception of 150 'bed case' wounded soldiers from the front. The military accepted the offer; the first patient arrived 31 January 1915.

Towards the end of the year, the rise in cot cases, led to Robb Brothers Ltd, of Grange Road, Birkenhead, converting two delivery vans into ambulances. The 'Vulcan' was known in the Red Cross transport service as the 'Robb' ambulance, the larger four-stretcher 'Albion' was named 'Sutton House' after the stores staff residence.

Other civilians contributed to home defence by joining the now almost forgotten civic volunteer battalions. Following an inaugural meeting on 27 November, Lieutenant Colonel Ellis, a former 4/Cheshire major was appointed as commander of the Birkenhead and District Volunteer Training Corps. The members, all beyond military age, purchased their own uniforms, the less well-off applied for a grant from a locally raised £1,200 fund for equipment and rifles; each member paid a five shilling subscription. In December 250 men attended their first drill at the 1/4 Cheshire drill hall.

The risk of invasion remained an omnipotent threat driven home on 16 December 1914, when two German battle cruisers commenced a thirty-minute devastating and demoralising bombardment of Scarborough, during which seventeen civilians died and eighty were injured. The 'baby killers' of Scarborough then headed north, briefly shelling the fishing port of Whitby, and bombarded the garrisoned port of Hartlepool, where a further eighty-six civilians and seven soldiers died, and 424 were injured.

Instead of the much quoted 'the war would be over by Christmas' in reality it transpired 'the war was over here by Christmas' – and with no end in sight.

An early December photograph showing members of the Red Cross VAD Detachment with convalescent Belgian soldiers outside the Red Cross Hospital at 19 Palm Grove. The building loaned by Viscount Hythe opened 4 November, and was entirely staffed by the women's detachments and other voluntary workers (Cheshire VADs 40 and 50).

IS YOUR NAME on a ROLL of HONOUR ?

IF YOUR NAME goes down on your firm's Roll of Honour, it also goes on that mighty Scroll which records the names of all who have rallied round the Flag.

There is room for your name on the Roll of Honour.

Ask your employer to keep your position open for you. Tell him that you are going to the help of the Empire. Every patriotic employer is assisting his men to enlist, and he'll do the right thing by you.

Tell him NOW—

Your King and Country Want you——TO-DAY.

At any Post Office you can obtain the address of the nearest Recruiting Officer.

GOD SAVE THE KING.

CHAPTER 3

1915 – Deepening Conflict

In the absence of the predicted swift victory, the combatant nations faced a strategic quandary over the most advantageous location to deploy their forces. As a stalemate existed on the Western Front, Germany opted for an overtly defensive strategy in France and Flanders and concentrated on defeating Russia. The respite afforded the beleaguered Allied armies precious time to regroup and absorb inexperienced battalions now arriving from New Zealand, Australia, Canada and the dominions.

The lion's mane is created from the countries of the Empire

The Glory of a
Lion is his
Mane.

COPYRIGHT.

In response to civilian disquiet over German raids, the Royal Navy answered with a 24 January victory at the Battle of the Dogger Bank. This curtailed the German naval raids, but evidence of poor naval gunnery and ineffectual communications were again ignored.

Three days later two merchant ships were torpedoed without warning by *U20*, in doing so the old fashioned courtesy of preserving life at sea fell by the wayside. Perhaps it was a notification of intent for on 1 February Germany announced an unrestricted submarine campaign, and henceforth ships of any nationality would be sunk without warning. This was soon followed by the German declaration that the waters around the British Isles were a war zone.

On the home front, the difference between life and death was becoming increasingly arbitrary, the latest example of 'Hun

Rathmore Convalescent Home

frightfulness' occurred on 19 January when Zeppelin airships carried out their first successful bombing raid on Britain; more followed. Non-combatant civilians now risked death from air attack and naval bombardment. On 12 February 1915, Birkenhead air raid precaution lighting regulations were instigated, lights had to be either reduced or shaded or made invisible from above. Illuminated shop fronts, lettering and powerful lights, including motor car headlights, were prohibited. Now largely forgotten, the 'black out' precautions are today more associated with the Second World War.

Military hospitals were mushrooming throughout the nation. In mid January, Oaklands Auxiliary Hospital admitted a dozen patients. This West Kirby auxiliary hospital was situated in a former merchant house and financed by West Kirby residents. By 11 December the hospital had treated almost sixty wounded men.

Prominent benefactors of wounded or sick soldiers were Mr and Mrs Harding of Noctorum, a suburb of Birkenhead, who resided in an imposing 1880s Jacobean-style residence built by Edmund Kirby. Their home 'Rathmore' was made available throughout the war to convalescing service-men.

During an early February meeting in Chester Castle, representative gentlemen from throughout Cheshire discussed forming a county regiment made up of battalions from each Parliamentary Division, they in turn being formed of companies from the several towns and villages in the county. On formation they would be affiliated with the Central Association of Volunteer Training Corps, whose headquarters were in London.

'Garn! you said it stood for 'Good Runners'—I don't believe it.''

The committee agreed to endeavour to raise several Volunteer Training Corps throughout Cheshire. About this time the existing Birkenhead and District Volunteers Training Corps became the Birkenhead Battalion Cheshire Volunteer Regiment.

By March, despite the national need for 'every shoulder at the wheel', industrial disputes throughout the nation were prevalent, the contributing factors being unscrupulous employers and discontent fuelled by war inflation. The strikers received little sympathy and were castigated from pulpit to trenches.

In a late March letter to his wife, Sergeant Major E. Owens, of B Company 1/Cheshire wrote:

> *'There has been nothing more or less than ten hells knotted into one going on here, but thank goodness, we have got things fairly quiet at present. I must have the devil's own luck. I am keeping in fine trim and up to the pink.*
>
> *'It is a pity that all those chaps out on strike at home could not be bundled out here: it would soon stop all the bother. Both masters and men are absolutely doing their level best to throw us over, and they are playing into the hands of the Germans. What they are doing is just what the Germans want. The Germans tried to get South Africa to rise, then India, and they thought Ireland would have struck for Home Rule. They have met with failure, and then England comes along and plays into their hands. It fairly makes me mad to think of it. I hope Kitchener takes things up firmly.'*

Meanwhile, on the Western Front, the arrival of spring stirred the Allies into action. On 10 March the British attacked the Germans positioned about the French village of Neuve Chapelle. British and Indian troops attacked on a 4,000 yard frontage capturing the village and several lines of trenches. But a shortage of artillery shells and German counter-attacks prevented a breakthrough. After three days the battle died away as the captured ground gained at the expense of 11,500 casualties was consolidated.

A special Red Cross train from Southampton delivered 200 of the Neuve Chapelle casualties to Woodside station where the local branch of the Red Cross removed the wounded to a long string of ambulances and motor cars, the task expeditiously carried out under the direction of Mr Roland Jackson and R. Shepherd. The majority of patients were taken to Tranmere Military Hospital and the annexe in Devonshire Place, also to 96 Liscard Road, West Kirby, Parkgate and Heswall.

Financing the diverse range of community run hospitals or nursing homes proved something of a financial headache. Despite the War Office hospital accommodation payment of two shillings per bed per day, fundraising events were essential. Planning for one of the largest fundraisers began in mid March when a joint committee of the Liverpool Theatrical, Gala and Liverpool Cyclist Committee met to discuss a Union Jack Day charitable collection in aid of the various institutions catering for wounded soldiers and sailors. The idea originated with Councillor W. Kelly, who had previously raised £1,900 on Belgian Flag Day. Kelly said he had come at great inconvenience, owing to the fact that all his theatre hands had gone on strike. Other meetings followed, including a well-attended ladies meeting in the Assembly Rooms in Birkenhead Town Hall where Mr Kelly explained the arrangements and the target figure of between £4,000 and £6,000.

Meanwhile the ongoing Merseyside dock workers' dispute was about to receive the intervention of Lord Kitchener. On Sunday 21

Woodside Ferry Terminus, the station is on the extreme right

March, Kitchener attended morale-boosting martial reviews in Liverpool and Manchester. From the steps of St Georges Hall, Kitchener, Lord Derby, Alfred Bigland, civic dignitaries and military staff officers reviewed 12,000 locally raised New Army troops. Before leaving for Manchester, Kitchener in his capacity as Secretary of State for War, held a brief meeting with the leaders of the National Union of Dock Labourers. Kitchener impressed most forcefully the dangers which were being caused by congestion of work at the docks.

In Birkenhead the ongoing gas strike continued, but labour from

Cheshire Bantams and other volunteers limited the impact of the strike. The strikers at the Municipal gas works wanted a four shilling (20p) a week increase on top of their twenty-six shillings pay for working a fifty-six hour week. In comparison, a Liverpool gas works paid twenty-eight shillings for fifty hours work.

During the 27 March Union Jack Day, 4,200 ladies sold miniature flags of special design in the streets of the various districts. Three quarters of a million flags were sold, bringing in over three tons of copper coins equating to £4,075 gross, of this Birkenhead raised over £714, Wallasey £382 and Port Sunlight almost £92.

The Bromborough community was also fundraising towards a Red Cross hospital within the club house of Bromborough Golf Club. The operating theatre equipped hospital would cost annually an estimated £500 over the government grant to maintain, but £352 had already been subscribed. Mrs E. Carter of 'Brookhurst', Bromborough successfully appealed to the public to donate a large amount of goods to furnish the hospital and under her leadership the hospital flourished.

The town's gas strike continued, but the latest Birkenhead dock dispute ended when *The Birkenhead Advertiser* published the dock workers' case. Their intervention appeased the workers, together with

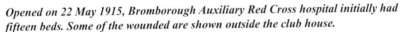

Opened on 22 May 1915, Bromborough Auxiliary Red Cross hospital initially had fifteen beds. Some of the wounded are shown outside the club house.

employer assurances of 'when the emergencies have been met and congestions are a thing of the past, a more favourable attitude would be adopted by employers'. But, an increasingly frustrated Lord Derby conducted a meeting in Liverpool and addressed a room brimming with dock workers. Derby explained he had two aims, to alleviate delays in the docks and to allow over-age men, including himself, to serve king and country, in which capacity he would serve as commanding officer of the battalion. As a result the 'khaki dockers', the 1st and 2nd Dock Battalions of the King's Liverpool Regiment were formed. Attempts to implement the scheme at Birkenhead failed for a considerable period; nonetheless, other ports also introduced dock battalions.

Also doing their patriotic duty on the home front were the volunteers of the Birkenhead Voluntary Training Corp who objected to having to purchase their own uniforms from a specified tailor, but once the issue was resolved the 'Dad's Army' in their Norfolk jackets took on a distinct military appearance. On Easter Monday, three companies of the Birkenhead VTC, mostly attired in their new uniforms had their first route march, their destination being Thornton Hough. The companies involved were A Company (Oxton), B Company (Rock Ferry) and C Company (Port Sunlight). Due to Bank Holiday work commitments D Company (Mersey Railway employees) were unable

The Birkenhead VTC on the march

Cheshire Volunteers
Cap Badge

to attend. After inspection by Colonel Sykes, they were put through various exercises and at 5pm the companies returned home headed by the 4/Cheshire band.

During mid April, the War Office acquired Hemingford Street Council School for use as a military hospital. Due to the building's design few modifications were required other than the installation of lifts. The pupils were transferred to Woodlands School.

At St Margaret's Road, Hoylake a small VAD hospital had opened on 1 February and had already admitted 110 men of the 16th (Reserve) battalion of the King's Liverpool (16/King's). According to the standard reference book on the subject, the 16/King's were formed December 1914, at Hoylake, but they were billeted at West Kirby Hall and the village Christian Institute. In early March the defended port battalion was completed by the arrival of five officers and 152 NCOs and men from the Isle of Man. In July 1915 the battalion departed to

Hemingford Street school, now Hamilton Buildings where the basement served as a mortuary, the lead- lined shelves are still in place, a part of the basement is unusually cold. Ironically, the flag is at half-mast in respect to Drummer Lee Rigby brutally murdered in London.

David Lloyd George

Kinmel Camp, Rhyl and thereafter the hospital received sick and wounded from the front.

The home front infrastructure may have been progressing nicely but British industry responded lethargically to the clamour for artillery shells. Following *The Times* reporting of the Neuve Chapelle shell shortage, the pressure applied by the Conservative Party brought about the collapse of the Liberal Government. The new coalition government established a Ministry of Munitions under the auspices of David Lloyd George. On 21 April he stated:

'During the fortnight of fighting in and around Neuve Chapelle almost as much ammunition was spent by our artillery as during the whole of the two and three quarter years of the Boer War. The urgent need for the country, then, is for shells, shells and more shells. ...A radical change of organization is necessary and it must be carried out at once.'

He was also a long term supporter of the Temperance movement; in March 1915 he famously stated: 'We are fighting Germany, Austria and drink'.

In an attempt to break the Western Front deadlock, Britain controversially launched an Anglo-French campaign against the Turkish army at Gallipoli. Anglo-French warships attempted to force the Dardanelles Strait to open up the supply route to Russia's Black Sea ports, but they suffered a humiliating defeat. On 25 April, the Allies made amphibious landings on the Gallipoli shores; bedevilled from the outset by inept leadership, the campaign ultimately became a military fiasco.

Meanwhile on the Western Front, near Ypres the Germans deployed their latest example of frightfulness – poison gas; but their attempt to break the deadlock failed. Throughout the year the British attempted

Ionic St. Auxiliary Military Hospital.

to wrest insignificant villages from the German invader, the battlefields of Loos, Neuve Chapelle and the Ypres salient rapidly attained their own notoriety for the war weary soldiers of 1915.

As the casualties mounted the 16/Cheshire vacated their Ionic Street School billet which became a military hospital, this being commemorated to this day by the inclusion of a red cross in the centre of the school uniform badge. The 16th Battalion camped at the Meols picnic site, where sea bathing and tented accommodation gave a holiday-like atmosphere. They remained beside the sea until 20 June when both Bantam battalions departed Wirral for Masham, near Ripon where the 35th (Bantam) Division assembled.

The men and women of Merseyside traditionally followed a seafaring career. Some of the most illustrious shipping companies were based in Liverpool, including Cunard whose 30,000 ton transatlantic line RMS *Lusitania* still steamed regularly between New York and Liverpool, confident in her ability to outrun any surfaced hostile submarine. On 7 May, as the vessel sailed fifteen miles off the Irish coast, she was torpedoed by the German submarine *U20*. The liner sank in minutes and 1,198 perished including 124 American citizens.

A
German Naval Victory

"With joyful pride we contemplate this latest deed of our navy. . . . ."
Kölnische Volkszeitung, 10th May, 1915.

This medal has been struck in Germany with the object of keeping alive in German hearts the recollection of the glorious achievement of the German Navy in deliberately destroying an unarmed passenger ship, together with 1,198 non-combatants, men, women and children.

On the obverse, under the legend "No contraband" *(Keine Bannware),* there is a representation of the *Lusitania* sinking. The designer has put in guns and aeroplanes, which (as was certified by United States Government officials after inspection) the *Lusitania* did *not* carry; but has conveniently omitted to put in the women and children, which the world knows she *did* carry.

On the reverse, under the legend "Business above all" *(Geschäft über alles),* the figure of Death sits at the booking office of the Cunard Line and gives out tickets to passengers, who refuse to attend to the warning against submarines given by a German. This picture seeks apparently to propound the theory that if a murderer warns his victim of his intention, the guilt of the crime will rest with the victim, not with the murderer.

News of the sinking initiated a series of riots in London and Liverpool, the orgy of retribution against Germanic businesses also erupted in Birkenhead. Vastly outnumbered, the police were either powerless or indifferent to the pillaging and arsonist intent of the mobs. According to *The Birkenhead News:*

> *'There was a resentful deliberateness running through all the shop wrecking, and the prime movers in most cases were women, women the wives and relatives of the stokehold crews of British liners who rightly or wrongly... stubbornly determined to take the law into their own hands.'*

The 12 May edition of *The Wallasey News* reported-:

> *'The violent disorders in which Liverpool set an example during the weekend spread to Wallasey on Monday, when rioting took place in the south end of the borough and attacks were made by angry crowds on establishments supposed to be carried on by Germans or suspected of having German connections. A pork*

The above picture of 35 Oxton Road, Birkenhead shows the destroyed pork butcher's shop of Charles Dashley. The German owner Karl Deuschie, anglicised his name when he arrived here in 1896, his former shop is now a repair centre.

purveyor's shop in Victoria Road, Seacombe and a butcher's premises in Poulton Road were both wrecked; great havoc was done at a fountain-pen factory at the corner of Desmesne Street and Chapel Street, and the residence of the proprietor in Somerville, was damaged as was also, in a lesser degree, a private dwelling house in Albemarle Road. In other localities there were demonstrations of a minor sort, but the damage was confined to the Seacombe end of the district. The police were powerless to afford effective protection to the establishments, though about 100 special constables were called out to their assistance, being conveyed in motors to where they were likely to be of most service. In two cases the mob invaded premises...'

The rioting may well have run its course when Birkenhead Mayor A.H. Arkle issued a sympathetic proclamation mentioning...

'playing into the hands of the German nation, since all the cost of the destruction has to be paid by the communities at large, all the 'silver bullets', we have will be wanted to defeat and demolish our enemies...'

The retribution against Germanic pork butchers may have disguised civilian disquiet over meat shortages. As food became less obtainable a West Kirby butcher remarked 'we can't get the meat because so much is wanted for troops in training'. The resulting high prices and scarcity of meat resulted in Birkenhead butchers mutually agreeing to close half a day on four consecutive weekdays.

Amid the locality's comings and goings were the Crosby raised 10th (Reserve) Battalion Prince of Wales' Volunteers (South Lancashire) Regiment. Stationed in the Deeside village of Heswall since the previous December, they now departed for Kinmel Camp, near Rhyl.

Locally their absence was offset by increased numbers of wounded patients; to meet the demand Wallasey Red Cross opened a hospital at the end of Atherton Street, New Brighton and adjacent to St George's Mount.

During the third week of May, the Dowager Duchess of Westminster, the president of the Cheshire Red Cross, visited and inspected Penkett Road Hospital. She then departed to officially open the Cenacle hospital and met the staff and sixteen patients.

The gothic style property originally known as 'Sand Rock' had a succession of wealthy owners, in 1912 the detached house and grounds were purchased by a French religious order the Convent of our Lady of the Cenacle (cenacle being an upper supper room symbolic of the Last Supper). The site is now St Peter and Paul's church.

As the conflict deepened, factories and communities endeavoured to boost war relief funds and satiate the ever-increasing demand for war munitions, prompting Lever Brothers to place part of their factory at the disposal of the Liverpool War Munitions Committee.

The war workers were not discernible from men avoiding military service, these 'shirkers', scorned at every opportunity, drew the attention of indignant ladies who would present a white feather or shower the stay-at-home in white chicken feathers. Unfortunately male munition workers received the same treatment. To prevent the social castigation of those 'doing their bit', in early 1915, the Government issued a 45mm high oval brass lapel badge for male Ministry of Munitions workers.

But there was no mistaking the 1/4 Cheshire who

had left England five weeks previously to join the Mediterranean Expeditionary Force. On 8 August, they and components of the 53rd (Welsh) Division landed at Suvla Bay, Gallipoli where they were almost immediately thrown into action. Ill-equipped with no knowledge of the terrain or dispositions of the enemy, they were thrown into battle, their orders being simply – attack the Turks. Despite their gallantry, the division's baptism of fire was an unmitigated disaster.

The alarming casualty levels were counter-productive to voluntarism and now, due to waning recruitment, the government appointed Lord Derby to implement a system of compulsory military service. The first steps towards conscription involved a national canvas to ascertain how many eligible men were in war service occupations or were avoiding military service. The first targets of the Derby Scheme were single men with no dependents.

Volunteer officials instructed the heads of families how to fill in the forms; those failing to comply were heavily fined. The government believed excessive drinking was detrimental to industrial output and contributed to high absenteeism. They considered introducing the

This postcard image of the British Red Cross Society (Wallasey) Division VAD featured in the 14 August 1915 edition of The Wallasey News.

contentious prohibition of alcohol, instead reduced licensing hours were introduced and beer was diluted in strength. Effective from 15 August, it became an offence under DORA for licensed premises to supply intoxicating alcohol to any NCO or soldier who was a patient of any military or auxiliary hospital in Western Command.

The war years were a transitional period for women and rigid social barriers began to crumble in pursuance of efficiency for the war effort. Female socialites appeared willing to fraternize with those well below their social status. Breaking new ground were the first six Birkenhead lady tram conductors, but new-found equality did not extend to pay; at the outset the ladies became a target for manure throwing youths, this ceased after dire warnings from the law.

During the hours of darkness the police remained vigilant for exposed lights from household windows, the Deeside police in particular kept the magistrates' courts supplied with a stream of offenders who generally received a five shilling (25p) fine. More truculent offenders received a ten shilling fine or the option of six days'

This image taken outside Rathmore is a good example of the walking wounded (seating) patients and a disabled cot case in a bath chair. The invalid perambulators were a common sight around town for they enabled the immobile to attend the many forms of daytime entertainment freely provided for the wounded.

imprisonment. Whether at leisure or work the state controlled the civilian population as never before.

Throughout the war Cammell Laird shipyard reverberated with the din of riveters as the yard produced a steady stream of fine warships, merchant ships and engines. This significant contribution to the war effort relied on the productivity of the work force whose attendance was carefully monitored. During a mid-September session of the District Munitions Tribunal at St George's Hall, Liverpool it was stated that during the past twenty weeks Cammell Laird had lost over 1,500,000 working hours. As the yard employed an average of 10,300 workers the lost time equalled a three-week shut down. Cammell Laird had issued sixty-nine summonses against their employees on a charge of idleness and losing time. A third of the platers, smiths and electricians pleaded guilty and were prosecuted under the Munitions of War Act 1915. The attendance and productivity of all munitions workers was continually monitored throughout the Great War and munition tribunals featured regularly in the press.

Another patriotic lapel badge of the period was the Admiralty war service badge introduced in 1914, for shipyard munition workers, the date remained unaltered throughout the war.

During March the British Red Cross Society and the Order of the Hospital of St John of Jerusalem invited mayoresses to participate in a 'town's ambulance' scheme to finance an ambulance for the front. Birkenhead instigated a fund on 1 May, a week later they had £707. Encouraged by the response, the mayoress opened a fund for a second ambulance, within four months the funds raised were sufficient for two ambulances.

In late May, Wallasey launched a shilling (5p) fund, this being the minimum donation to the 'town ambulance' fund, within a fortnight £600 was raised. Audience collections and donations from various music-halls and picture houses in the borough took the total to £1,110, sufficient for two ambulances.

A 'town ambulance' bearing the Birkenhead borough coat of arms and town name.

Wallasey Corporation decided to emulate Liverpool's mid June establishment of a Munitions of War Committee. This resulted in a section of the ferry workshops being dedicated to the production of artillery shells under the direction of Captain W.H. Fry, the manager of Wallasey Ferries.

Sourcing the required machinery proved difficult due to demand, as even used machines proved exorbitantly expensive, these were sourced from industrial centres throughout the country. The difficulty of power was overcome by tapping the tramways circuit and by the purchase of a traction motor of forty horsepower intended for the South-Eastern and Chatham Railway Company. Within the small space the difficulties of arranging efficient drive belts without causing congestion on the floors was overcome. With no model to work off and, barring one private machine shop, a total lack of experienced machinists, four supervisors were brought in from Oldham who also acted as tool-setters and tool-makers. In addition a woman charge-hand supervised every twenty operatives.

The plant turned out 500 preliminary shells a week and, as the

Unskilled women soon developed into efficient shell production workers. This munitionette lathe worker is turning shells

workers acquired skill, output increased and six months later 900 shells per week were being produced. It was then decided to introduce female labour and to undertake additional operations. Excluding four male supervisors and two other men working the parting-off machine, the munitionettes produced at least 970 shells a week, but these were all subject to critical inspection.

During the autumn Lever Brothers responded to a request from Lloyd George's Government and undertook shell production. The Port Sunlight repair workshops were immediately utilized, additional machinery was manufactured together with the necessary gauges for shell construction.

On 25th October the first delivery of shells was made, production continued until the end of June 1916. The works and their associated companies ultimately produced two-thirds of the war-time glycerine used for explosives by the British Army.

The company research laboratory discovered a toxic gas known at the front as PS (Port Sunlight) gas. Produced on a large scale by the military authorities it was used prior to the introduction of mustard gas.

The average infantryman earned one shilling a day plus a graduated separation allowance paid to his dependents. Ellesmere Port working class dependants are shown waiting for their payments.

Others were far removed from penury, probably including local gentlemen who submitted in October 1915, a proposal for the establishment of a Hoylake munition factory. They offered to defray the cost of fitting out and hand over to the Liverpool Munitions of War Committee any factory profit; this was the first of the non-profit making factories to be established in the Liverpool region.

The factory was established in an existing motor garage close to Hoylake station. It was divided internally by timber partitions, which formed rooms for inspection, bond rooms and other offices. A canteen and separate buildings with toilets for men and women were erected; the latter had the novelty of hot and cold running water. Initially the enterprise was primarily run by volunteer labour, but these were replaced by female labour. The workers machined various types of shell up to the point of preliminary inspection; the further finishing operations were carried out at the Lambeth Road National Shell Factory. The factory was managed by Mr Harold Janion with a foreman in charge of each shift. In spring 1918 women were substituted for the foremen. The total Hoylake output was:

4.5-inch High Explosive shells - 63,841
18-pounder shells - 50,784
60-pounder shells - 6,575

The non-profit-earning factory was so successful that the directors were able to pay off all their capital charges and hand over nearly £20,000

Munitionettes stockpiling shell blanks supplied for machining

to the Liverpool Board of Management. Of this sum £12,000 was allocated to Liverpool University.

The 13 June 1919 edition of *The London Gazette* recorded the Hoylake and West Kirby Munitions Factory would be wound up voluntarily and that Harold Janion of the Club House, Hoylake, be appointed liquidator for the purpose of winding up.

By this stage of the war, recruitment numbers had gone into freefall, military personnel made 'enlist' appeals during musical halls and theatre intervals. The predicament was summarised when Captain Marquis announced to an audience: 'The casualties of 1/4 Cheshire since 24 August were 450, and to replace that number in the last seven weeks they recruited seven men.' But, as Derby's Military Service Bill began to loom, men attested (signed up) in order to select the regiment they desired and avoid the tag of being 'a conscript'. After attestation, the majority returned home to await their call-up papers. Others objected to conscription including the No-Conscription pacifist movement which viewed compulsory military service as a contravention of their religious belief and a form of national slavery. They successfully campaigned for a conscience clause in the Military Service Act.

In time, the pacifists might become involved in agricultural work alongside female workers. Several titled Cheshire ladies met at Crewe as the Cheshire County Committee for promoting the employment of women in agriculture and horticulture. It was reported that the training schemes in the public gardens were progressing favourably, and that women were being trained in the parks at Crewe, Heaton Park and Birkenhead. The returns for October showed that 107 vacancies for women farm workers and women gardeners had been taken, and sixty-six vacancies for women for potato picking had also been filled including those on Wirral farms.

On 8 October the Mayor of Birkenhead opened the new hospital annexe at 6 Manor Hill. The following month at Hoylake the local VAD of the British Red Cross, formed at the start of the war, responded to the military request to extend their accommodation for nursing wounded soldiers. To make this possible, Mrs Danby, who had a house 'New Bunnee' on Meols Drive, generously placed the house at the disposal of the Cheshire 120 VAD, together with the financial means

Manor Hill Hospital annexe

to make certain improvements. The hospital opened on Monday, 13 December, the commandant being Miss Redcliffe of West Kirby.

Also in December all men over fifty years of age in the Birkenhead Volunteers appointed themselves recruiting sergeants about the town. Men also aided the fire brigade, guarded the docks, kept air raid watch and helped man anti-aircraft guns. There was also a last minute local rush to attest to pre-empt the forthcoming introduction of Derby's Military Service Act – better to serve as a volunteer than a conscripted man.

One such volunteer Private B. Moore who was 'somewhere in France' driving the second Birkenhead ambulance, forwarded the following letter to the Mayoress of Birkenhead:

> 'Dear Mayoress,
> 'Just a few lines to let you know the car presented to the Red Cross Society by you on behalf of you and your citizens is going strong and doing very good work. As I am the driver of the car, I feel it is my duty to inform you where it is and of the good work it is doing. I know you will be pleased to hear of it, and you can tell your patriotic citizens the good news, and that it has been highly

appreciated by the many wounded it has carried, and that I am proud to drive it, as I am a Lancashire lad from Nelson. I will close now; hoping you get this letter.

'I remain, yours sincerely, Private B. Moore.

'P.S. The make of the car is a Buick, body built by Furnival of Birkenhead.'

As Christmas approached the surreptitious evacuation of Gallipoli commenced thus drawing down the curtain on the debacle of the Dardanelles campaign. Together with the remnants of the 53rd (Welsh) Division the 1/4 Cheshire departed for Egypt to refit and reorganize prior to engaging the Turkish army. Anglo-French forces were also embroiled at Salonika (now Thessaloniki); the first troops arrived on 5 October 1915 to oppose Bulgarian and German forces. The campaign continues to be overshadowed by events on the Western Front despite the presence of some 600,000 British, French and Serbian personnel.

Closer to home, Boxing Day witnessed the departure of six boys from the 7th and 12th Wallasey scout troop, who departed from

An embroidered silk postcard sent by Liscard man, Private Lesley Douglas Gillborne 13/Cheshire. The message reads:-'Xmas 1915. Wishing you the old, old wish, and a happy New Year. This is a monoplane of an -unknown make but made in 'Gay Paree'. Think of us at Xmas having roast turkey and plum pudding and an afternoon nap. Golly. France, December 1915. In the trenches.

Woodside Station to undertake coast-watching duty on the south coast. They were all first class scouts with signallers and ambulance badges. All were cyclists and four were experienced horse riders making them suitable for despatch work. Between them the scouts had thirty-two years experience, three having served over six years each. In common with other scouts on coast duty the boys received daily pay of 1s 6d (7.5p) and had to do their own washing and cooking. They too were leaving all that was dear and was probably there first Christmas away from home.

2nd (Birkenhead) Battalion Cheshire Volunteer Regiment

CHAPTER 4

1916 – The Realization

As the New Year dawned those reflecting on the previous year would have gained little consolation from the naval and military manoeuvres. The Western Front was frozen in aspic and the Royal Navy, colloquially referred to as John Bull's teeth, looked increasingly fallible. The realization dawned that the British Empire was embroiled in a war of attrition of which a British victory could no longer be guaranteed. Against this faltering military backdrop, the home front had evolved into an ever more productive supplier of all manner of essential products ranging from knitted gloves to battle ships.

The newspapers routinely reported on the arrival of wounded or the latest fundraising effort, but due to repetition and the constraints of space, the remaining chapters will focus predominantly on other home front activities. The introduction of the Military Service Bill or conscription became the topic of the day.

The Society of Friends (Quakers) and members of the Socialist Labour Party formed the 'No-Conscription Fellowship' and successfully campaigned for a conscience clause in the 1916 Conscription Act. On moral and religious grounds the 'conchies' or COs refused to break the sixth commandment 'Thou shalt not kill', no matter the circumstances.

The defiant men comprised three categories; the most obstinate were the 'absolutists' who rejected any form of alternative war service that supported war. They refused to take up arms or participate in innocuous and diverse employment encompassing building rifle ranges to sack making, for the end product could be for sandbags or coaling warships.

The middle category 'alternativists' also shunned weapons training and soldiering, but were willing to work in occupations not controlled by the army, typically agriculture.

The 'non-combatants' did accept military service but in a non-combatant role, several thousand serving in the Royal Army Medical Corps as medics or front-line stretcher-bearers. March 1916 saw the establishment by the army of the Non-Combatant Corps, dubbed the No Courage Corps by the press. The NCC were willing general labourers for any task except handling munitions.

Ultimately over 16,000 men claimed the right of exemption from military service. More than 6,300 COs were court-martialled and incarcerated. Over 800 spent more than two years in prison enduring privation, hard labour, no talking, a bread and water diet and brutality. The uncompromising regime led to seventy-three deaths, others left prison physically broken or mentally ill. Decades later, a variant of this press gang descendent would force other generations to a stint of

Nurses at Hooton Park Hospital

military service; British conscription was finally laid to rest in the 1960s.

But there was no rest for the hospital administrators who faced a financial uphill struggle tending the wounded as indicated below:

'Dear Sir,
The fine weather has done much for the men enabling them to get out in the fresh air. Their friends have been kind with invitations. I have to thank Dr and Mrs Brierley also Mr and Mrs C.B. Burrows. The men enjoyed themselves very much at each place. The Girl Guides under the leadership of Miss Bout, are doing a real service for us, undertaking the mending required. This is a great burden taking off the hands of those who are fully occupied in other work, and the Girl Guides are rendering efficient help to the cause we all have so much at heart.

Will friends who give cigarettes kindly give the money they would send to our matron's cigarette fund, as we are now able to get the cigarettes and tobacco free of duty for our men?

I want to make up subscriptions amounting to nine shillings weekly. This spread over a number of people, is not much to ask for, and I feel sure there are many who would like to help our work.

*Yours truly,
G.J. Townsend.
Commandant.
Oaklands.
27 January 1916.'*

Strident fundraising efforts were made to alleviate servicemen's hardships, the latest Birkenhead scheme being tramcar collections inaugurated in February 1916. The collections on behalf of local military units at home and abroad, local naval or mercantile marine (Merchant Navy), prisoners of war, the Red Cross society, YMCA Hut work, local hospitals etc raised over £3,021 in the inaugural year. By the time of the Armistice some £6,680 had been raised.

Thousands of wounded soldiers were invalided home for medical treatment or palliative care. For those who succumbed to illness or injury families either arranged internment in a private/family grave or those in dire financial circumstances settled on burial in a public or pauper grave. This shameful treatment of the fallen prompted Birkenhead Corporation to inter free of charge service personnel who died within the Flaybrick cemetery burial area including members of His Majesty's Forces who prior to enlistment were resident in the area. The cost of excavating and infilling the private section graves was borne by the burial authority, the communal graves later acquired multiple-named Commonwealth War Graves Commission screen wall headstones.

Until now the Zeppelin raids had concentrated on east coast targets, now Germany intended to show Britain they could penetrate the breadth of the country with impunity. On the night of 31 January nine Zeppelins loaded with incendiary and high explosives soared into the air and set a course for Liverpool, their objectives the flour mills and grain elevators on both sides of the river. Adverse weather, navigational problems and mechanical difficulties scattered the aircraft across the midlands. *Kapitänleutnant* Max Dietrich commanding *L21* was seventy miles off course when he mistook the lights of Derby for Manchester and the featureless Shropshire and Welsh countryside for the Mersey. Hampered by poor visibility, Dietrich mistook the lights of Tipton for Birkenhead and not realising he was north of Birmingham, he concluded the lights of Wednesbury were Liverpool. When the airships disgorged their payloads, sixty-one people died and a further 100 were injured.

In late February the raid resulted in the introduction of more adequate anti-aircraft measures. The Chief Constable of Birkenhead warned residents the town's electrical engineer would give warning of air raids by dimming the electric lighting and gradually shutting the lights off after ten minutes. The Ellesmere Port air raid alert was the sounding of the Shropshire Union fire buzzer and the gas (gas lighting was still prevalent) would gradually be turned off.

Regardless of the aerial threat and the prospect of invasion, thousands of voluntary clerical volunteers now applied themselves to implementing the compulsory call-up of various groups or categories of men. The first group called upon were single men and childless widowers between the ages of eighteen and forty-one who had attested under Lord Derby's voluntary attestation scheme. But the

administrators' unfamiliarity with the group system resulted in the March premature call-up of married men, instead of attested bachelors. An outbreak of protests resulted in the May introduction of a revised Military Service Act. Regardless of this, the systematic calling up of married men would inevitably have caused great concern to their dependents in an era when the male was usually the primary wage earner. The introduction of conscription ended the chicken hunt and men from a wide demographic now faced an uncertain future.

Those who believed they had reasons for exemption from military service could appeal to a tribunal; the Birkenhead tribunal first met on 12 January and would continue for almost three years. The Birkenhead

Unmarried.		Married.	
Age.	Group.	Age.	Group.
18–19[1]	1	18–19[1]	24
19–20	2	19–20	25
20–21	3	20–21	26
21–22	4	21–22	27
22–23	5	22–23	28
23–24	6	23–24	29
24–25	7	24–25	30
25–26	8	25–26	31
26–27	9	26–27	32
27–28	10	27–28	33
28–29	11	28–29	34
29–30	12	29–30	35
30–31	13	30–31	36
31–32	14	31–32	37
32–33	15	32–33	38
33–34	16	33–34	39
34–35	17	34–35	40
35–36	18	35–36	41
36–37	19	36–37	42
37–38	20	37–38	43
38–39	21	38–39	44
39–40	22	39–40	45
40–41	23	40–41	46

HOW I FELT BEFORE THE TRIBUNAL.

A postcard of a tribunal

Borough tribunal usually sat bi-weekly and dealt with approximately 6,000 applications which involved the completion and mailing out of between 30,000 and 40,000 forms. In total the Wirral tribunal held eighty-seven sittings, processed some 2,000 original applications and an unstated number of subsequent appeals.

On 17 March, the first local tribunals for conscientious objectors met, eleven days later the first Birkenhead conscript was charged for failing to present himself. Others seeking exemption were employed in starred or badge occupations, terms used for those working in wartime production roles.

The tribunal officials included a military representative and they rarely acted impartially. In most instances tribunals were simply a humiliating formality that might produce a temporary exemption, barely sufficient for an individual to wind up his affairs, but most stoically accepted the decision.

The police also had extensive powers, for example strangers writing down train or shipping movements were summarily arrested. Given the authorities' vigilance concerning any suspicious activities amongst the indigenous population, the latest restriction on non-British residents was introduced without a murmur. On 10 March under the Aliens Restriction Consolidated Order 1916, aliens of every nationality were notified after 13 March that they were forbidden to enter, be in, or reside in any prohibited area unless in possession of an identity book. These were available for one shilling from Birkenhead central police station.

The aliens were in an unenviable position, for throughout the country bereaved families began to commemorate their fallen relations, on 15 March a local newspaper reported on the first significant Wirral memorial. Captain Morton Brown Paton 10/South Lancashire was attached to 6/Lancashire Fusiliers. He died 7 August 1915, has no known grave and is commemorated on the Helles Memorial, Gallipoli. His brother A.V. Paton, a well-known cotton broker and West Kirby resident, donated to the National Trust an open space adjoining Thurstaston Common as a memorial to his brother and other fallen north Wirral men. The site was chosen for its likeness to Thurstaston Hill and Achi Baba, upon whose slopes Captain Paton fell leading his men in action, while the cliffs at Caldy beach closely resemble the

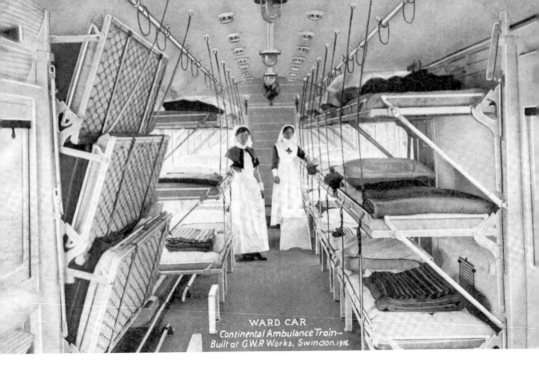

WARD CAR
Continental Ambulance Train—
Built at G.W.R Works, Swindon.1916.

beach on which the Lancashire landing was made. Today few ramblers are aware of the overall significance of the tranquil site.

As the war dragged on, the ambulance trains continued to disembark wounded at Birkenhead, and to meet the spiralling demand for beds more auxiliary hospitals and staff were required. In response, the Rock Ferry Men's VAD (Cheshire 31) was formed in October 1915 in

The Abbotsford (Rock Ferry) Red Cross Auxiliary Hospital operated from a detached house loaned by Mr C. May Massey. The hospital opened on 1 February 1916, and received its first patients on 10 May. The hospital closed down on 10 May 1919, having admitted 409 in-patients, and treated 20 out-patients.

connection with the Cheshire Branch of the British Red Cross Society. The thirty-eight men on the roll all gained their first aid badges in January and had attested for the army. The president of all Cheshire branches was Katherine, Duchess of Westminster, the Rock Ferry vice president being Miss Oakshott, its commandant Mr Leigh Oakshott, and Dr G.V. Oakshott the lecturer. The headquarters was at Abbotsford.

Volunteers were also active at Bidston where the exposed YMCA marquee had a tendency to collapse in high winds so a more robust structure became a priority. On 18 March, Gershom Stewart MP officially declared open, the spacious YMCA hut at Bidston Training Camp. The fully-furnished mock Tudor style structure cost £1,250, of which £1,050 had already been raised. Bidston residents and other friends financed the hut on the understanding that at the close of war the hut should be handed over to Bidston Church as a parish hall; it fulfilled this role until a fire in the late 1960s.

The YMCA hut at Bidston Hill

The YMCA also provided a hut at the Bebington Showground officered by a committee of local ladies. Opened on 4 March initially for the Bantams' use, throughout the war it continued to provide a service for other military units.

For a long period the YMCA ran Sunday teas from their Grange Road building (now Primark) later reducing to the first Sunday of the month. For three years in conjunction with the Sunday teas, a canteen for wounded soldiers operated, open every day from 2pm. It attracted 2,000 visitors a week. The YMCA was also prominent at Woodside Station.

When the Royal Flying Corps established a training aerodrome at Hooton Park, a YMCA canteen was established at Childer Thornton for the airmen quartered at Hooton Hall. There was also a Heswall tent and the Vittoria Dock Hut, opened on 11 January 1916, which provided refreshments for men working on the docks; refreshments were also provided at several lesser venues.

The YMCA workers were conspicuous wherever troops were present, but there was no hiding place for men attempting to avoid call-up, the latest amendment to DORA reinforced the message by imposing a minimum fine of five pounds on those failing to comply with the National Registration Act. The severity of the fine equates to a month's salary paid to the new female postal workers.

However, not everything was progressing in female favour, for the Convalescent Home for Women and Children in Rowson Street, New Brighton became an auxiliary military hospital. The military selected the premises due to the location being 'one of the healthiest and bracing spots in the United Kingdom' calculated to be most beneficial in restoring a soldier to health, the suitability of the internal arrangements and staff for the purpose of a garrison hospital, and the proximity of the home to the several large camps in the immediate neighbourhood. The hospital opened 17 May 1916, the accommodation comprising four beds for officers and seventy-six beds for NCOs and men.

Rowson Street Convalescent Home

A year later the AGM reported 640 military patients had passed through the hospital, the daily average of occupied beds being sixty-four. However, the hospital operated at a loss primarily due to inflation, the balance sheet showing the expenditure during the past year was £3,149, which was £776 less than the income. The receipts included

Women's On War Service badge

subscriptions £459, donations £100, army pay £1,461, the amount received from patients £279.

The war created unprecedented employment opportunities for females, as employers grudgingly conceded women were capable of more than domestic work. In late February, the Chief Constable of Birkenhead instigated a waged Women's Police Detachment and other traditional male bastions crumbled, as women swept streets and worked on public transport. Arguably the best remembered female workers were employed in the munition factories, where the munitionettes played an indispensable role in Britain's war effort. In May 1916 a brass brooch in the form of an equilateral triangle engraved 'On War Service' was introduced for female munitions workers and 270,000 were issued throughout the war.

Other ladies preferred more genteel options. In June 1916 another Cheshire Red Cross branch registered, the Women's VAD, (Cheshire 126) comprised 120 members, of these, twenty-seven were special nurses in military hospitals, eleven served as cooks, clerks and pantry-maids in other military hospitals; the remainder worked fortnightly shifts at Abbotsford under a sister-in-charge and the night nurse staff. Ten were employed in the kitchen.

By the end of June the government had mastered the inadequacies in munition production, and Lever Brothers' shells were no longer required. Since the previous October the soap maker had produced an average weekly output of 320 shells, making a total of almost 12,000. The percentage of rejected shells was only 1.6 which at that time was considered something of a record, the rejects being attributed to faulty material.

But, the munitions produced in government arsenals would prove singularly ineffective against armour plate when the German High Seas

Fleet was brought into action on 31 May, to the west of the Jutland bank, off the coast of Denmark.

British vessels had inadequate armour plating and fire control systems, consequently when struck by German shells the magazines on some vessels exploded. Poor gunnery, signalling and a lack of night training compounded the senior service's problems. Thousands of British lives were lost as warships exploded and sank in seconds. Included in the local deaths were Private James W. Price, Royal Marine Light Infantry, who was on HMS *Defence*, where there were no survivors. Stoker J. Williams of Abbot Street was lost in the tragically dramatic sinking of HMS *Tipperary*. Another lost warship HMS *Warrior* had until recently been under repair at Cammell Laird, and the yard built HMS *Chester* which is forever associated with the youngest recipient of the Victoria Cross.   Boy First Class, John Travers Cornwall VC was mortally wounded early in the action, the 16-year old remained standing alone at his exposed post, quietly awaiting orders, until the end of the battle with the gun's crew dead and wounded all around him. Arguably at Jutland there was no tangible victor, a viewpoint that continues to be debated.

Commemorative Medal

The training ship HMS *Conway* (ex HMS *Nile*) was for many years moored in the Mersey off New Ferry. Launched in 1839, the sailing

HMS Conway training ship

H.M. TRAINING SHIP "CONWAY"

ship was a twin deck, second rate ship of the line equipped with ninety guns. Renamed *Conway* in 1876 the wooden walls reverberated to the sound of youths receiving instruction in the art of seamanship. At the time of Jutland the training ship held a record number of 228 cadets. *Conway* established a fine reputation as a source of potential maritime officers; nine old boys were killed at Jutland. An impressive service was held onboard in their memory during which Mr Killey, the chairman of the *Conway* committee handed a laurel wreath interwoven with white lilies and bearing the *Conway* colours to Captain Broadbent and Mr Barr the chaplain, then dedicated it to the memory of the ship's heroes.

Another naval disaster occurred on 5 June, when HMS *Hampshire* struck a mine off the Orkneys. Amongst the dead was fading national hero Lord Kitchener who was heading to Russia for a conference.

Among the home front's unsung heroes were the Girl Guides who gave invaluable assistance in Red Cross hospitals, made bandages and knitted large numbers of socks and gloves. They, like the scouts, worked in gardens growing home produce, collected waste paper for the war effort and raised funds to provide some home comforts for those serving overseas. When Cheshire Girl Guides aimed to raise £500

A postcard commemorating the death of Lord Kitchener.

for a soldiers' recreation hut for France, the nineteen Wirral companies raised almost £66 of the required sum. Throughout the conflict, old-fashioned Wirral hospitality was also extended to personnel based in the region.

In early June in the grounds of West Lodge, West Kirby about fifty minesweeper crew from Liverpool and wounded soldiers from the Chalet, Hoylake were entertained. The tearooms were decorated with messages of welcome by a display of signal flags, which greatly pleased the company. After a high tea, they were entertained with old English sports on the lawn, concluding with a billiard match between the army and navy. The lady voluntary workers, headed by Miss Crowther of the Hoylake Munitions Works together with the chaplain of the Mersey Mission to Seaman, received the highest praise for the way they arranged the races. After the prize giving, light refreshments followed, then the naval men left in time to catch the 9.10 train for Liverpool while, the wounded soldiers from the Chalet were driven home.

However, any servicemen unwilling to 'do their bit' received no sympathy, especially from non commissioned officers who had served overseas and possibly received incapacitating wounds. Lance Corporal Barker was such a man, his mistreatment of conscientious objectors prompted a 19 June telegram to the authorities and full enquiry.

Private Carradice arrived in Prees Heath camp under escort and was placed in the guardroom where he stated 'that he was a conscientious objector and could obey no orders'. The next day he was ordered to turn out for parade and refused to do so. Lance Corporal Barker seized him by the back of the neck and ejected him. As he would not march anywhere, Barker cuffed him along. Carradice was next taken to the bath cubicle and on refusing to wash was roughly handled by Barker. The case for Private Ingham was similar. The commanding officer stated that these men, with five others, were seen by him on arrival. They refused to answer any questions and were disrespectful in manner and stated they were conscientious objectors. He consequently directed they should be handed over to a good disciplinarian.

The enquiry determined Barker performed his duty, but as he had crippled fingers it was considered physically impossible to strike severe blows. He was disciplined and was not to be put in charge of other conscientious objectors; any future instances of insubordination were to be forwarded to a district court martial.

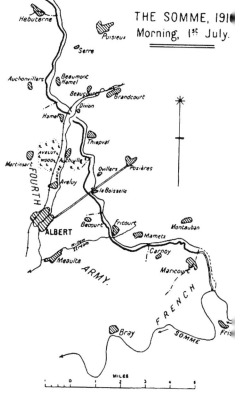

THE SOMME, 191(Morning, 1st July.

All of Britain was alive with talk of the impending 'Big Push' on the Western Front. Neither the timing nor the location were to General Haig's liking but, as the junior partner in the Franco-British alliance, Haig had to bow to the French demands for a major British offensive to divert German troops away from the siege of Verdun.

On 1 July, the opening day of the British Somme offensive 21,392 soldiers were killed or missing presumed killed. Approximately 40,000 more were wounded or maimed and many would die from their wounds months or years later.

The offensive was the first taste of battle for Kitchener's citizens' army including the Liverpool Pals who shared the laurels in the costly capture of Montauban, one of the day's few gains. A week later they attacked and captured the natural stronghold of Trônes Wood, the survivors being relieved on 13 July.

On 3 July the 11/Cheshire (25th Division), which contained a strong element of Wirral men, were tasked with capturing Thiepval. However, inadequate communications and confusion resulted in a three-hour postponement of the infantry attack – but not the artillery support. The shelling had severed telephone lines so the orders for the new barrage had to be carried by runners, who in the darkness and congested state of the trenches made slow progress. Most of the batteries received the revised orders too late, fresh orders were being drafted when shell fire caused the loss of forty key personnel in Brigade Headquarters. However, an advance was made with little infantry support, the 11/Cheshire *were met by a withering fire of machine guns, under which they walked forward till the battalion simply melted away.'*

Due to the catastrophe, reinforcements poured into the Somme area including the 35th (Bantam) Division destined to support the woodland fighting on Bazentin Ridge. On 16 July, the 16/Cheshire took up position in the recently captured Trônes Wood, their brother battalion being deployed in nearby Bernafay Wood. During this period, the division rarely fought as a complete unit, instead they were utilised in various other brigades. The 35th Division incurred severe losses during trench digging or actions attached to other infantry divisions where the lifeblood of the 104, 105 and 106 Brigade Bantams flowed freely. Replacements for the lost 'short but wide men' were no longer available, on 25 August a draft of casualty replacements was rejected as being unfit for military service. But, despite the low grade replacements the bantams continued to be thrown into battle.

For every infantryman killed in battle four or five would be wounded, some fatally, an already overburdened hospital system in France and Britain received a deluge of Somme casualties. The conveyance of the casualties from Woodside station to auxiliary hospitals over-stretched the available ambulances. On 26 July Birkenhead held a flag day to finance another ambulance for use in Birkenhead; this effort and others raised £1,400 sufficient to purchase the transport and allocate £500 towards its upkeep.

The authorities generally accepted whatever benefactors offered, although there was some reticence in accepting the generosity of Mr William E. Cain, the chairman of Robert Cain and Sons Ltd. In March, the brewery magnate offered his West Kirby mansion 'Wilton Grange', as a 'Home of Honour', for soldiers

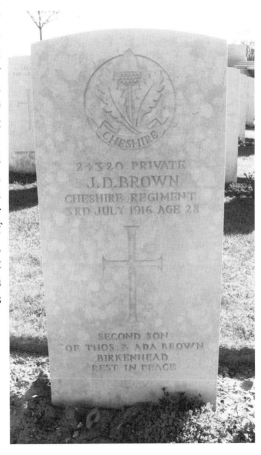

Private John Duff Brown serving with C Company 11/Cheshire died 3 July. Unusually his parents included his home town 'Birkenhead' on his Lonsdale cemetery headstone.

The ambulance was presented and dedicated to Chief Transport Officer Rowland Jackson in recognition of his work with the wounded and their distribution to hospitals.

totally disabled in the war. In August, after five months deliberation, the offer was declined; this may have been due to the Cain source of income – intoxicating liquor. In October 1918 Wilton Grange became a convalescent home for army officers. Some prisoners of war were adopted by schools or societies who responded to prisoner's correspondence by forwarding requested goods, the infrastructure for delivery being highly efficient. At home, the wounded benefitted from a full programme of gratis entertainment in theatres and teetotal establishments and in the summer months the local community arranged trips to the country or the seaside with its invigorating sea breezes. The Wallasey ferries *Iris* and *Daffodil* did their share of excursions for the wounded. Both boats would later receive their own wounds from bullet and shells incurred in action.

As the Wallasey ferries plied their trade they steamed past the almost completed Wallasey Town Hall, where work was being carried out at the expense of the War Department to adapt the premises for use as a temporary military hospital.

The Medical Officer of Health, Doctor Barlow, had general control of the arrangements. The Wallasey branch of the Red Cross Society undertook to carry out the transport work in connection with the hospital. Sitting patients were carried in private cars, but stretcher patients required an ambulance. In Wallasey they had only one ambulance, presented by Doctor McDonald, and one trailer besides the borough ambulance which was required for local needs.

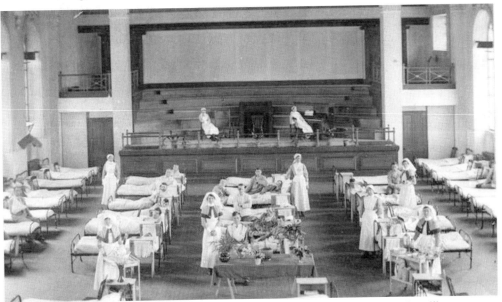

On 12 and 13 August, the public were afforded the opportunity to inspect the military hospital. At first the hospital provided accommodation for between 325 and 350 wounded for whose reception the building was opened almost immediately.

A public meeting was held in the Town Hall on 16 August with the object of raising £1,000 to purchase three ambulances. That night a committee of ten was formed and between them they contributed £165 to the fund. In nine days public contributions swelled the fund to £400, after a favourable treasurer's report two ambulances were ordered on 24 August, delivery being expected in three to four weeks. When the fund passed £750 an order was placed for the third vehicle. The fund received an unexpected bonus from New York where Alexander D. Wood, of Allerton Road, Wallasey was stationed as a shipping company Marine Superintendent. Having read of the ambulance appeal in *The*

The chapel in the town hall hospital

Wallasey News, Wood collected £135 in subscriptions. In ten weeks the fund received £1,400, sufficient for three ambulances, leaving over £350 towards running costs. The vehicles would greatly alleviate the pressure during the transportation of wounded from Woodside station.

Military discipline continued during the soldiers' sojourn in hospital. A 12 September letter to *The Birkenhead News* by a 'Tommy's friend',

Woodside station, on the right of the image, was the terminus of the GWR and regularly received ambulance trains from the south coast and Liverpool, via Runcorn; the Wirral bound wounded detrained here.

Ferry Approach, Birkenhead

highlighted disconcerting discipline in an unidentified military hospital based in one of the largest schools in Birkenhead, where wounded soldiers had to be in by 6.30pm in comparison with the others of between 8 and 9pm.

> *'Patients must not go within six yards (5.4m) of the railings. Seats are to be removed to the back of the yard. Parcels and letters must not be passed through the railings. Any patient infringing this order will be liable to be treated as a defaulter. Signed Matron.'*

The editor replied: 'There are obvious reasons why patients in our military hospitals should be forbidden to receive promiscuous parcels'. This brought about a reply from 'Indignant' concerning the childish treatment meted out to the gallant inmates of Temple Road military hospital.

> *'Last Saturday a hockey match was arranged at Seacombe. As the soldiers were entertained for tea there, it was impossible for them to be back by the absurdly early regulation time of 6pm. The consequences of them being late was that their clothes were taken from them and they were not allowed out of bed on Sunday.'*

It is assumed the situation was promptly remedied.

On 17 August Mr Edwin Montagu, Minister of Munitions, reported to the Commons on the improved output of munitions. The production of 18-pounder shells had risen to 170 times, and in heavier shells 2,650 times, greater than at the start of the war.

In an attempt to break the deadlock on the Somme, and contrary to modern opinion General Haig did embrace new tactics and technology. On 15 September, Haig launched the Flers – Courcelette advance, it was the first time tanks were used on the Western Front. Both villages

The 33mm diameter sterling silver war badge was instituted from 12 September for men who had served at home or abroad since 4 August 1914, and who on account of physical infirmity arising from wounds or sickness caused by military service have relinquished military commissions or, in the case of other ranks, been discharged. The badge could only be worn on civilian clothing and was worn on the right breast, normally on a jacket lapel; there would be no shortage of eligible candidates for the badges.

were captured despite the tanks suffering from mechanical failure or becoming bogged down, but the potential was there; within days Haig placed an order for 1,000 of the new weapons.

But the wonder weapons had failed to break the impasse consigning the British to further bloodshed in renewed offensives. The infamous Somme battles continued until mid-November when 'General Winter' forced a seasonal postponement of military campaigns.

THE SOLDIER AND THE SONG

A little bird sang in a leafy tree,
And he sang his song right merrily.
Oh, a blithesome song 'twas all day long,
To the tramp of men he sang his song-

To the tramp, tramp, tramp of the soldier.
A little bird sang in a leafless tree,
But he sang his song less merrily.
The summer was there, but the tree was bare,

And poisonous gases filled the air,
And the tramp, tramp, tramp of the soldier.
A little bird lies at the foot of a tree,
Lies dead on the breast of a soldier.

Oh, sweet little bird did your song take flight,
With a soldier's soul in the dead of night?
Will it cheer his way to the realms of bliss-
To a brighter, better world than this-

To the Home of the war-worn soldier?
Oh little bird, oh little bird where have you gone,
Far away with our soldier son;
Far away with your own sweet song,

Far from the tramp, tramp, tramp of the soldier?

George Manson.
25 Mossy Bank Road,
Egremont.
11 October 1916.

The offensives might have halted, but shells fell with the monotony of a dripping tap, and casualties were supplemented by snipers who had honed their art to deadly perfection. Men returned from the horrors of

A King's Liverpool soldier outside Rathmore. He wears the regulation hospital uniform of a blue suit with white jacket lapel facings and red tie.

Conscientious objector postcard

the trenches minus an amputated limb, suffering from debilitating illness or shell-shock, now recognised as post traumatic stress.

In mid October, questions were asked in the House of Commons concerning further ill-treatment of Cheshire Regiment conscientious objectors during exercises in Birkenhead Park. On hearing of this Mr H.W. Forster for the Secretary of State for War promised a full enquiry into whether the ill-treatment happened as a result of an order by Major Rodney, after a demand for a court martial had been refused. Once irregularities were established, the three privates were arrested pending a military court martial.

Shortly after the park incident, the 30 October *The Liverpool Daily Post and Mercury* reported the story of an Enfield conscientious objector who was sentenced to death in France and was currently serving a commuted sentence of ten years penal servitude. At the Middlesex Sessions, Enfield builder Herbert Runham Brown, a member of the No-Conscription Fellowship appealed against a staggering £50 fine for issuing circulars contrary to DORA.

The circular reproduced a letter from his friend G.H. Stuart Beavis, who had been arrested as a conscript. On 3 May, Beavis and other conscientious objectors were taken in handcuffs to France.

'Dear Mother, We have been warned today that we are within the war zone, and the military powers have absolute power. Disobedience may be followed by severe penalties, and very possibly the death penalty, so if I just drop you a line in case they do not allow me to write tomorrow. Do not be downhearted. If the worse comes to the worst, many have died cheerfully for a lesser cause.'

The circular suggested readers should write to Mr Asquith and others and implied the men would be shot even though the sentence had been commuted. Major Wilson, Assistant Adjutant General for London, explained the circumstances in which the death penalty might be inflicted at the front. If a man refused to mend a necessary road fifteen miles behind the front and thus prevented it being used for some time or, if in refusing any task he assisted the enemy or jeopardised the lives of his colleagues, he might suffer the death penalty. The appeal was dismissed with costs and the court refused to reduce the fine.

Doing just fine were members of the Liverpool Regiment whose heroism drew praise from a British staff officer who spoke of the mysterious tanks, in particular 'Birkenhead', which was temporarily attached to the Liverpools:

'During an advance it stopped short of the enemy's trench, and remained silent out in no man's land. The enemy thought it had broken down, and they came rushing forward with great glee to catch the monster. They were allowed to creep very close. Then the Birkenhead began to spit death. The enemy, scared out of their wits, flew like frightened rabbits. The Birkenhead kept blazing away at the fleeing Germans and started off in pursuit of them. The Huns were outclassed, and when Birkenhead got to work properly, the enemy surrendered to the Liverpools. It thrills one to think that Birkenhead keeps up a fair name out there.'

Another Birkenhead connection withered on 6 December, when the 35th Division lost its Bantam status and would in future accept standard height men as, due to a shortage of manpower, all battalions were now accepting shorter men. By the end of December a series of inspections had reduced the 35th Division by a quarter, as 2,800 men were rejected as physically unsuitable. The root of the problem stemmed from

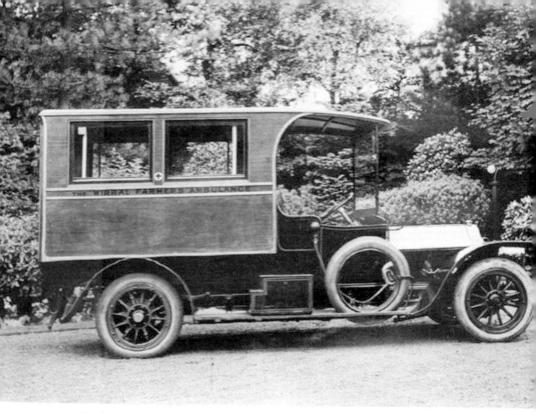

During 1916 fundraising for ambulances continued, at the beginning of December, this ambulance, financed by the Farmers of the Hundred of Wirral, became the latest to be presented to the Red Cross. A standard ambulance carried four stretcher cases or eight sitting wounded.

military depots forwarding immaturely-built men who would previously have been rejected. In a war of attrition too many of these men were directed to the Bantam division.

On 13th December, Lieutenant Colonel Arden presided over a district court martial held at the 3/Cheshire Birkenhead headquarters to enquire into charges made against four soldiers – Acting Sergeant Fred Marshall, Lance Corporal Cheers, Corporal Williams and Corporal J.W. Williams of ill-treating two conscientious objectors, Privates Dukes and Beardsworth, during gymnastic exercises in Birkenhead Park.

Captain Rimmer prosecuted and Mr Russell Roberts (Messrs Hill, Dickinson and Co,) appeared for the defendants. Captain Rimmer pointed out he was at a disadvantage, an escort had been sent to a detention camp where Dukes and Beardsworth were confined and informed the two men they were to attend the court martial, but they both refused to attend.

"IS YOUR SON GETTING ON ALRIGHT
IN THE ARMY ?"
"YES. I THINK SO, HE SAYS HE'S IN FOR
A COURT MARTIAL "

Acting Sergeant Fred Marshall was charged with ill-treating a soldier on 22 August by forcibly compelling Charles Dukes to execute certain gymnastic exercises by using unnecessary force, thereby causing him pain and suffering. The defendant pleaded not guilty to the charge and to a second similar charge of ill-treating Private George Beardsworth.

Corporal Robert Baker said he was in Birkenhead Park on 22 August in charge of a gymnastic parade when Dukes was brought to him by the accused and Corporal J. Williams and was put through gymnastic exercises directed by these two, he saw no ill-treatment. This was contrary to another witness who, on 27 August, saw Dukes's injuries. The lower parts of his legs and ankles were discoloured and swollen, the cuts and bruises seemed to be the result of being thrown on the ground.

With regard to Beardsworth, his wife said she was in the park on 31 August and was standing at the gate near the water fountain as her husband was being taken over the obstacles. Beardsworth refused to go over the vaulting pole and they threw him over. At the water jump he refused to leap and they pushed him in. Five or six unidentified men then threw him over the escalading board, this was repeated a second time, an officer said 'stand clear' and her husband fell. He was then taken to the inclined plank and told to walk up it, but he refused. After several attempts they shoved him up, and at the end they doubled his body and he fell off head over heels. On 3 September her husband was black and blue all over.

Several defence witnesses denied there was any violence used including Mr Russell Roberts. After a lengthy adjournment Marshall was brought before the court and found not guilty of the charges against him. Owing to Dukes's absence Corporal John William Williams was acquitted of charges of forcibly cutting Dukes's hair and ill-treating soldiers in the park. Lance Corporal Cheers was also acquitted due to Beardsworth's absence.

Appearing in a different kind of dock were men of the 15th (Transport Workers) Battalion South Lancashire Regiment, who were formed in December for work in Birkenhead docks. The following April in Preston the regiment raised the 16th (Transport Workers) Battalion who also worked in the Mersey docks.

As the third wartime Christmas approached, George V issued the following messages to his soldiers, sailors and the sick and wounded:

I send you, my sailors and soldiers, hearty wishes for Christmas and New Year. My grateful thoughts are ever with you for victories gained, for hardships endured, and for your unfailing cheeriness. Another Christmas has come round and we are still at war. But the Empire, confident in you, remains determined to win.

May God bless and protect you. George R.I.

TO THE WOUNDED

At this Christmastide the Queen and I are thinking more than ever of the sick and wounded among my sailors and soldiers. From our hearts we wish them strength to bear their sufferings, speedy restoration to health, a peaceful Christmas and many happy years to come.

George R.I.

Christmas Dinner for the patients in Wallasey Town Hall

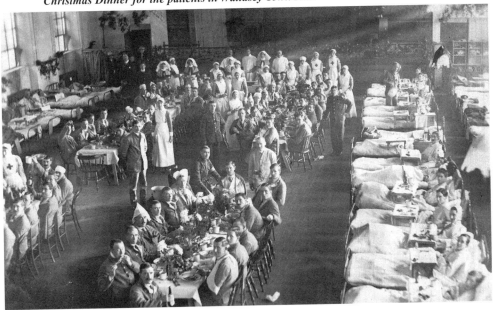

Wallasey Auxiliary hospital menu. As the Christmas festivities rapidly approached the community ensured the wounded were not forgotten.

CHAPTER 5

1917 – Seeing it Through

The subjects of Kaiser Wilhelm II of Germany were equally bowed and blooded and committed to a war of attrition. The Kaiser and George V were grandsons of Queen Victoria, but the warring cousins now had something else in common, their subjects faced food shortages. Britain's two and a half year distant naval blockade of German ports had a severe impact on food imports and war materials, however both cargos clandestinely passed through neutral ports. On the other hand the Royal Navy were at their wits' end on how to deal with submarines preying on the merchantmen, Britain's maritime trade links were becoming increasingly endangered.

In December, German attempts to negotiate a peace settlement were dismissed by the Allies, this rejection combined with the blockade, brought about a catastrophic shift in sea policy. The German government proclaimed from midnight 31 January no Allied vessels would be permitted access to a Barred Zone extending from a line drawn from Flamborough Head to Terschelling, an island off the Netherlands, and between Ushant off the Brest Coast and Land's End. Territorial waters of neutral countries were observed, but any vessel entering the prohibited waters of the North Sea or the Atlantic near the British Isles faced destruction.

As food shortages proliferated the nation began to 'Dig for Victory,' by utilising sections of municipal parks and waste ground. At the start of January, in response to requests from the Food Controller, the

Wallasey Parks Committee recommended the following lands be temporarily utilized as allotments:

1. The land south – east of the lake in Central Park. (13 plots).
2. Recreation ground Central park abutting upon Poulton Road. (105 plots)
3. The Wallacre, Wallasey Road. (206 plots)
4. Captain's Pit, Mount Pleasant. (16 plots)
5. Flynn's Piece, Grove Road. (24 plots)

Volunteers digging

And subject to the consent of the Health, Education and Works committees, the following:

6. Land adjacent to hospital, Leasowe Road. (50 plots)
7. Land off Valkyrie Road. (54 plots)
8. Braddofields, Claremount Road (about 2,800 yards)

Total number of plots (exclusive of Braddofields) 468, of an aggregate area of 30 acres.

The 300 yard plots were rented for five shillings or £4 an acre and Wallasey purchased a steam traction engine for ploughing the grassed fields. Neighbouring Birkenhead rented allotments for fifteen shillings and tenants faced the back-breaking job of removing turf prior to cultivation.

In late January, despite unfavourable weather, a number of Cheshire Volunteers were busy trenching the ground at St Andrew's road, in preparation for potato cultivation.

Birkenhead Corporation and private allotments amounted to seventy acres, an acre being divided into sixteen plots. A further fifty acres were now scheduled for allotment purposes, they were:

1. Derby Park, New Chester Road.
2. New Chester Road, opposite the abattoirs.
3. Bedford Avenue and Albany Road.
4. North and south sides of Bedford Drive.
5. Part of Victoria Park.
6. Mount Road.
7. Corner of Temple Road and Borough Road.
8. Temple Road.
9. Corner of Woodchurch Lane and Storeton Road.
10. Part of Arno recreation ground.
11. Bidston Road opposite St Saviours' Church.
12. Mather Road.
13. Shrewsbury Road by All Saints' Church.
14. Corner of Park Road South and Slatey Road.
15. Tollemache Road.
16. Boundary road by King George's Way.
17. North side of Bidston Avenue.
18. Lansdowne Road and Summer Road.
19. Birkenhead Park, the plot known as Booth by Estate.
20. Lot 6 of Birkenhead Park land (Ashville Road).

The Dell nursery land was also under consideration. With 120 acres returned to soil 1,920 allotment holders toiled away in food production.

Not to be outdone, Hoylake had eighty-seven allotments, West Kirby had fifty-three and Meols had sixteen. The railway companies patriotically allowed residents to work land adjoining the railway track from West Kirby to Caldy, consequently eight plots were cultivated at West Kirby plus six at Hoylake.

On 1 February the German Government announced that it would 'henceforth tolerate no hospital ship' in defined areas and would, contrary to the Geneva Convention, treat hospital ships as legitimate targets. The neutral Americans were becoming increasingly fractious. Following the German decision to conduct unrestricted submarine warfare, America severed diplomatic links with Germany, thus taking a minute step towards war. From mid-March American merchant ships followed the Anglo-French lead and commenced fitting their merchant ships with stern-mounted defensive guns.

On Saturday 6 February General Sir W. Pitcairn Campbell opened a new ward and day room at the Neston Red Cross Military Hospital. The new ward could accommodate eleven patients and could be converted into a then in vogue open-air ward. The day room adjoined the new ward and was supplied with up to date heating and electrics.

A week later, on a delightful Wednesday afternoon a large number of invited guests were invited by the officer in charge Mrs G.J. Carter to view the extensions made to Bromborough Auxiliary Red Cross Military Hospital. The extensions comprised a well-appointed recreation room, several huts with beds for staff, a private office for the commandant, and kitchen extensions. Also the accommodation included an operating theatre and two wards respectfully named the Pitcairn Campbell and the Hathaway in deference to General Sir W. Pitcairn and Surgeon-General Hathaway (of Western Command) and also an open-air veranda, bathrooms and kitchens. All told the hospital now had 100 beds; this, according to Mrs Carter, made Bromborough the largest Wirral Red Cross hospital.

A nutritional balanced diet was essential for the speedy recovery of the wounded but the most basic ingredients were becoming increasing difficult to purchase, especially potatoes.

Given the dearth of the humble potato, profiteers attempted to

This postcard depicting a queue for potatoes parodies the popular 1914 song
'There's a long, long trail.'

exploit customers, despite a government order regulating food prices. At Birkenhead court a retailer appeared, accused of selling 2lb of potatoes to a customer for 4d, thus exceeding the maximum price of 1.5d per pound allowed by the order. The bench fined the defendant 30s or 16 days jail, the chairman pointing out that he had broken the law. However locally, due to the potato famine, there was little business being carried on.

Unlike in France, where from the last week in February, German forces began a tactical withdrawal to the Hindenburg Line, a system of supporting fortresses in parts some twenty miles (32 km) to the rear of their original front. As they covertly withdrew they operated a scorched earth policy, poisoned water supplies and destroyed the infrastructure.

At the same time in Mesopotamia (Iraq) the British launched an offensive in the direction of Baghdad. Also in March the King George V, still fearful of invasion, appealed to his subjects not on military service to either join the volunteers or be categorised as vulnerable as women and children.

In the House of Commons, the First Lord of the Admiralty reported that in the first eighteen days of the month 134 British, Allied and neutral ships were lost and described the submarine menace as grave and the problem still unresolved.

On land gains were made on the Somme, and the British captured Baghdad. Another British force, in what became known as the First Battle of Gaza, unsuccessfully attacked the Turkish province of Palestine. It would take until December before the British, including 1/4 Cheshire, entered Jerusalem.

In Russia deep-rooted social tensions exacerbated by shortages of food and fuel paved the way for revolution and the 15 March abdication of Tsar Nicholas II. Amid increasing concerns over Russia's willingness to prosecute war on the Eastern Front, on 9 April the British attacked German positions in Artois, east of Arras. The first day gains included the capture of Vimy Ridge by the Canadians, but at Bullecourt it would take days to pierce the Hindenburg Line and the advance gradually became deadlocked and dragged on to early May.

At sea the Germans carried out their threat to sink a hospital ship. *Asturias* formerly of the Royal Mail Steam Packet Company was the

HMHS **Asturius**

largest cross-Channel hospital ship, having cots for 895 patients. Shortly before midnight on 20 March 1917, as she steamed off the Devonshire coast mercifully with no wounded onboard, *Kapitanleutnant* Walter Schweiger (who sank the *Lusitania*) fired a torpedo from *U20*. The explosion blew the stern off the ship, destroyed the engine room and plunged the ship into darkness. Despite the damage HMHS *Asturius* managed to beach herself. Germany justified their first deliberate attack on a hospital ship by alleging the British used the vessels for carrying munitions in breach of the Geneva Convention. The international symbol of the Red Cross no longer guaranteed neutrality.

The county of Cheshire had ninety-four Red Cross work parties. In July 1916, a return was asked for the previous seven months' work – no fewer than 140,000 articles had been made and despatched to various hospitals and distribution points.

The Work Depot at Birkenhead, under the leadership of Miss E.U. Cunningham, during the January to June 1916 period, produced 24,987 articles. Special mention was also made of the Hoylake, Heswall and Hyde Comforts Funds.

THE KING'S MESSAGE.

"I am confident that all who are now prevented from undertaking active service abroad will join the Volunteers, and show to our enemies that my subjects of all ages are ready to serve in the defence of our beloved country."

George R.I.

WILL *you* answer the King's appeal by giving up a portion of your spare time for training to defend *your home?* We can only feel ourselves fully secure if every available man is trained to meet any emergency which may arise. In case of invasion trained men take their place in the firing line or on lines of communication—*untrained men have to go with the women and children.*

DON'T HESITATE—JOIN THE

2nd (Birkenhead) Battalion
Cheshire Volunteer Regiment.

Lt.-Col. M. C. ELLIS V.D. Commanding.

You will find good comradeship and every facility for interesting and instructive training. You will be trained under Army Instructors. The Battalion has the use of four miniature rifle ranges and also possesses a fine band.

Join whichever Company you find it most convenient to train with

"A" (OXTON) COMPANY.

Headquarters: Drill Hall, Grange Road West.
Officer Commanding, Capt. W. H. RICHARDS.

"B" (ROCK FERRY) COMPANY.

Headquarters: The Gymnasium, Nelson Street.
Officer Commanding, Lieut. GRAHAM JONES.

"C" (PORT SUNLIGHT) COMPANY.

Headquarters: The Auditorium, Port Sunlight.
Officer Commanding, Capt. W. HULME LEVER.

"D" (MERSEY RAILWAY) COMPANY.

Officer Commanding, J. SHAW, Esq.
(Confined to the Staff of the Mersey Railway.)

Apply by post card for further particulars to the Officer Commanding any of the above Companies.

L. H. MOSELEY,
Lieutenant and Adjutant.

GOD SAVE THE KING.

March 1917

King George V's March 1917 message

During eight weeks of unrestricted naval warfare, over 500 merchant vessels were lost at the start of the great shipping annihilation, and the arrival and departure of neutral cargo vessels plummeted to a quarter of the equivalent months in the previous year. The Western Approaches became a graveyard for ships, German predictions of starving Britain into surrender within five months looked increasingly likely. Evidently the Royal Navy anti-submarine tactics comprising offensive patrols and barrages across the English Channel and the Mediterranean Otranto Straits were ineffective. Sighting a U-boat, never mind sinking one, proved exceptionally difficult, for submarine detection technology was still in its infancy.

A sailing ship about to be scuttled by the U-boat crew

The Admiralty opposed the traditional wartime safeguard of escorting merchant men, but in February, pressure from Admirals Jellicoe and Duff brought about the first 'modern age' controlled sailings (or convoy) by escorting colliers to France. By the end of May, only nine of the 4,000 coastal ships using the system had been sunk. And, on the evening of 10 May, the initial homeward-bound convoys departed from Gibraltar and the United States of America. Their successful United Kingdom arrival led to the August implementation of the convoy system. Mercantile shipping losses of twenty-five per cent in February steadily reduced as more escort vessels became available and by the end of the year the losses were a sustainable one per cent.

In their quest for more soldiers, the Government summoned all previous military rejects for re-examination, but bone-fide agriculturists were excused, for by now only six weeks of corn supply remained in the country. Householders converted lawns to vegetable plots. Also engaged in part-time food production where the employees of Allansons one of Grange Road's larger retailers. The now predominately female staff cultivated an allotment in Storeton Road to the left of the Prenton tram terminus. The 1,300 yard plot was sub-divided into four sections each worked by a squad of fifty-five ladies. The gardeners were credited with the hours worked and received a commensurate share of the crop or payment corresponding to the market value of the produce.

Their dividend paled into insignificance against the 3.2 billion dollars of American exports shipped to the Allies throughout 1916. Spurred on by rogue attacks against American vessels, on 6 April 1917, President Wilson received approval to declare war on Germany, followed by a 7 December declaration against Austria-Hungary.

In mid April, the French General Robert Nivelle launched a major offensive between Soissons and Reims, a distance of approximately forty miles (64 km). The majority of the personnel were tasked with capturing the series of densely-wooded ridges, forming the Chemin des Dames. German artillery fire and entrenched machine guns decimated

On 14 May during a visit to the region, King George V and Queen Mary visited Cammell Laird's shipyard. The oil painting by artists Arthur James Wetherall Burgess and Edward Frank Skinner captured the royal visit and included portraits of prominent people, not forgetting three munitionettes clearly visible in the bottom left corner. The painting is included in the Williamson Art Gallery and Museum collection, Birkenhead.

the French and the offensive resulted in deadlock. Having sustained some 187,000 casualties, with their self-esteem shattered, some French front line units mutinied. With the French army in meltdown, the offensive was aborted on 9 May. Until the French morale recovered the British had no recourse but to engage the enemy at every opportunity.

In the United Kingdom morale of the Cheshire Volunteer Corps was certainly in the ascendancy. Following vigorous winter training in Wallasey, the battalion again assembled at their headquarters behind Liscard fire station. Despite men recently being absorbed into the army the battalion still mustered 550 volunteers. On an early May Thursday evening the battalion paraded in Central Park to be inspected by Lieutenant General Sir E.A.H Alderson KCB, until recently in command of the Canadian Corps in France, and now Inspector General of Infantry attached to the Western Division. The Wallasey battalion had been selected from the county battalions for this honour. The men acquitted themselves so well as to win strong expressions of approval from the distinguished general. After the inspection the companies marched off to allocated spaces, where displays were given in bayonet fighting, company drill, bombing, entrenching, signalling, musketry and ambulance work. The duly impressed visitor departed as the region prepared for a fleeting royal visit.

In the same month another armaments works innocuously came into production. His Majesty's Explosive Factories were located throughout the nation. Work commenced on the Ellesmere Port chemical works in

Manor Hill Staff, 26 May 1917

May 1916. The Cheshire plant being created for the production of synthetic phenol, from which picric acid was derived. This chemical was the primary high explosive ingredient used in the production of artillery shell explosives. The first Ellesmere Port output was in May 1917, production continued after the armistice to replenish ammunition reserves.

As the food crisis heightened, George V signed a proclamation exhorting people to lessen their consumption of wheat and to practise the greatest frugality in the use of all types of grain. Families were encouraged to reduce their consumption of bread by one quarter and those who kept horses were forbidden to feed them oats or other grain unless they had a specific licence from the food controller. The king also requested all churches to read the proclamation each Sunday for four successive weeks.

On 24 May at Charing Cross, Birkenhead's Mayor read aloud the king's proclamation on food economy and the Wirral War Agricultural Committee surveyors began to select land for wheat production.

In parts of Wirral the presence of glacial till (clay) affects the permeability of the underlying strata, consequently in bad weather fields flood. The water drains through many tributaries of the River Birkett which ultimately channels flood water into the Great Float. This Birkett head is arguably the origin of the name for Birkenhead. With every acre of land now required for the plough, the Cheshire War

EAT LESS BREAD.

THREE SLICES AMONG FOUR OF US
THANK GOODNESS THERE'S NO MORE OF US.

Agricultural Committee received a request for 150 German prisoners to be employed on the Birkett improvement scheme in the interests of food production.

The Wirral Union Area District Sub-committee met at Hooton. On 6 June, the secretary read out a letter from the Chief Constable of Cheshire concerning employment of prisoners of war in the prohibited area of the Wirral Division:

> '*I have to inform you that I consider such prisoners of war should only be admitted in the prohibited area under a strong military guard, with sentries who should always be mounted over batches of prisoners.*'

He proposed using the catering pavilions at Moreton and Barnston as prisoner accommodation and stipulated the number accommodated at each site must not exceed seventy-five. He calculated the military guard on seventy-five prisoners would require thirty-five NCOs and men. The committee accepted some of his advice and on 23 August German prisoners of war commenced work on the Birkett scheme.

In West Flanders, British engineers were also busy, driving twenty tunnels (the Germans discovered one) towards Messines Ridge, south of Ypres. This natural stronghold, held by the Germans since 1914, dominated the British lines until 0310 hours on 7 June when nineteen mine heads crammed with 600 tons of explosives blasted the Germans off the ridge. The next day German counter-attacks were repulsed, subsequent counter-attacks decreased in intensity and by 14 June the British held the entire ridge and delivered a desperately needed boost to national morale, removing a key obstacle to an impending British advance.

Most early twentieth century citizens held strong religious beliefs and these manifested themselves in street shrines, the forerunner of the wider community-financed war memorials. In the first week of July the first war shrine in the north of England was unveiled. The shrine in Silverlea Avenue, Liscard was in the form of a wooden tablet secured to the wall of one of the houses and contained white paper under a glass covering, the names of a large number of those, presumably connected with St Mary's parish, who had fought and died in the war. Some four weeks later, the Birkenhead Mayor unveiled the town's first war shrine located by the road bounding St Paul's churchyard, Tranmere.

Factories and social clubs were also commissioning rolls of honour to the fallen, but these required regular amendments as the casualties rose. They were once prevalent but the vast majority of temporary memorials, like the men commemorated, have long gone. Also forgotten are the individuals who considered it their duty to improve the lives of the local wounded, including Laddie who, with a little help, had by this stage raised £130.

On the Western Front a fortnight-long British preliminary bombardment involving 2,000 field guns and 1,000 howitzers pulverised German defences across eighteen kilometres of front in

Laddie was the archetypal butcher's dog, whose master was a well-known tradesman of Oxton Road. On joining the forces in January 1916, Private John Connor, who was attached to the 3/South Wales Borderers, had to close his business and, in his absence two policemen became the dog's guardians. Laddie, wearing a saddle-type collection box, rendered valuable services to many causes, this picture taken in late July depicts Laddie and PC Brooks fundraising for the VAD at Charing Cross – to stand there now would be suicidal.

Staff of Hemingford Street Auxiliary Military Hospital 5 May 1917

readiness for the Third Battle of Ypres. As an indication of Britain's ability to bite back, the barrage expended some 4.24 million shells.

On 31 July, the officers' whistles blew, and the men went 'over the top' to meet their destiny. Despite Haig's meticulous preparations to capture Belgium ports occupied by Germans, early successes foundered against in-depth German defences, and then Germany's ally – the rain – intervened. The bombardments had destroyed the watercourses, flooded shell holes became death traps, streams burst their banks, and the ground became a quagmire, paralysing the advance of British, Canadian and Australian troops. But they stoically pressed on in the mistaken belief the Germans were on the verge of collapse. The notorious offensive continued for several months, culminating in the battle of Passchendaele. The fight for the village continued until 6 November when Canadian troops entered the demolished village, the British offensive then ceased.

Despite the parlous predicament of the war-weary infantrymen, conscientious objectors continued to refuse to submit to military service and 1,219 were held in civil prisons. The latest inmate was

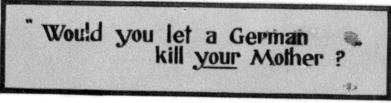

At tribunals this question was frequently put to conscientious objectors

Private Fred Shaw of Liscard who was sentenced at Chester to 112 days imprisonment with hard labour, for refusing to obey an order from a superior officer. On completion of their sentence, determined prisoners of conscience again refused orders, and the cycle resumed.

More willing military participants were the members of the Women's Army Auxiliary Corps (WAAC) formed in early 1917, for duties other than nursing. Some 6,000 members of the Women's Legion worked in army kitchens, camps and canteens or filled male roles as motor drivers, store-women, telephone operators and a myriad of other functions and it became obvious that a co-ordinating organisation was required. The WAAC arose from a combination of the Women's Legion and all other societies concerned with women's army work. The following year nearly 40,000 women had enrolled including some

A lot of fellows in the Army chew gum— but some prefer W.A.A.C.'s

7,000 who served in the rear areas of the Western Front filling roles that released men for front line duty, albeit on a reduced pay scale than their male counterparts. The women's section of the National Service scheme also comprised the Women's Land Army, the VAD and the Timber Section.

The ambulance trains continued to trundle into Woodside station, the 22 August Birkenhead News reported the arrival of a further 448 wounded men.

On Monday evening a hospital train arrived at Woodside station conveying 216 wounded soldiers for distribution amongst hospitals of the district. And, in the early hours of Wednesday another train arrived bringing 233 more cases.

The Monday evening patients numbered 120 cot and 96 sitting cases, and they were distributed thus: Cot cases: Tranmere Hospital, 87; Borough Hospital, 22; Manor Hill, 8; Arrowe Hall, 3. Sitting cases: Thornton Manor, 16; Neston, Parkgate, Hoylake and Wallasey, 20 each.

The 233 Wednesday arrivals, all sitting cases, were conveyed to the following destinations: Hemingford Street, 40; Mersey Park, 20; Ionic

Mersey park auxiliary hospital staff, 28 May 1917

Street, 40; Temple Road, 33; Neston, 12; Thornton Manor, 12; Hoylake, 20; Wallasey (Town Hall) 40; Wallasey (Penkett Road), 16. The anxious families of the wounded were, for now, spared the arrival of a loved ones final letter.

HIS LAST LETTER
Only a line on paper,
All dirty crumpled and torn,
Which a dear lad sent from the trenches,
Before the battle morn.

Only a number, only a name,
Amongst the thousands on the scroll,
Who fought the fight, who played the game,
And paid to death the toll.

Only a line by a dear one sent
The night before he died,
But it comforts the mother, when grief is spent,
And her sorrow is fortified.

M.D. Candlish,
Liscard.
1 September 1917.

In the nineteenth century, Welsh migrants, principally from North Wales greatly contributed to Birkenhead's expansion and cultural development. On Wednesday, 5 September 1917, the Welsh Eisteddfod

The grand main entrance to Birkenhead Park

Gorsedd (a coming together of a community or bards) commenced in Birkenhead Park.

The next day the nation's most eminent Welshman, Prime Minister David Lloyd George, arrived and was greeted by an enthusiastic gathering including 600 munition girls from Port Sunlight who stood in a long line along outside the pavilion waving flags and cheering lustily as the procession progressed along Park Road North.

After the customary speeches, the Prime Minister received a commemorative gift and the Freedom of the Borough of Birkenhead, all this was overshadowed by one incident.

Prior to announcing the champion of free verse, the prize, an intricately carved throne-like chair was brought to the front of the platform. *The Birkenhead News* reported:

'Around the chair gathered Archdruid Dyfed and the Gorsedd Recorder who called upon "Fleur-de-Lys" to answer the call that being the nom-de-plume of the competitor who had been awarded the Celtic chair. But, alas there was no response. The successful competitor had answered a greater call than that of Archdruid Dyfed; he had fallen in France in freedom's cause. The chair – which had been presented by David Evans and designed and executed by Eugeen Vanfleteren, [a Belgian refugee residing in Birkenhead] was enveloped in black. Dyfed – in Welsh and English – informed the vast and silent audience of the sad reason for the action.'

The winning bard, 61117 Private Ellis Humphrey Evans served with 15/Royal Welsh Fusiliers. The eldest of eleven sons to hill farmer parents, he enlisted in February 1917, in lieu of one of his younger brothers who was called up. The poet shepherd was killed on 31 July during the advance on Pilckem Ridge near Boesinghe, Belgium and features in the author's *Battleground Boesinghe* book. The chair passed into the keeping of the soldier's family and remains in the former family home in Trawsfynydd, Merionydd; the North Wales farmhouse is now owned by the National Trust.

Further upriver, at Hooton Park a Royal Flying Corps aerodrome was established for air training. During 1917, the site underwent transformation, the racetrack became a landing strip and three double and one single adjoining hangers, barracks, workshops and ancillary

Throughout the conflict numerous 'wounded river trips' occurred. The photograph shows some of the 350 wounded during a 13 September river trip sponsored by a Noctorum gentleman. The wounded were transported to Woodside landing stage by members of Cheshire 19 VAD, quickly transferred to the ferry Bidston *and placed comfortably on deck. Music was provided by the band of the Liverpool Orphan Asylum who interrupted a short Heswall holiday. The sailing ship on the left is probably* Conway.

buildings were constructed. The hanger roof timbers were of Belfast Truss design, a form of lattice-work incorporating economical lengths of timber, thereby eliminating the need for long timber joists but still providing a span of almost 80 feet (20m). The spans abutted each other delivering a total span of 160 feet and an obstruction-free area for housing aircraft.

On completion in September 1917, the site became Number Four Training Depot Station (4TDS). Assorted aircraft operated from Hooton including Avro 504 trainers, Sopwith Scouts and Sopwith Camels. The first trainee pilots were British and Commonwealth, followed by American and Canadian aviators. Mechanical failures and inexperienced pilots made a lethal combination. St Mary's churchyard at Eastham contains the remains of at least seven men from 4 TDS, including four Canadians and one American.

Coincidently another local flying victim is buried in Hendon (St Mary) churchyard. Second Lieutenant John Daniel George Brendel served in the Canadian Militia prior to joining the Royal Flying Corps. On 27 December 1918, while flying near Eastham he is believed to have fainted and his plane crashed into the River Mersey. An eye witness stated:

> The machine appeared to be doing a spinning nose-dive, which developed into a straight nose-dive. When the plane was near the water there was a noise like a pistol, this probably came from the engine.'

The experienced 27-year-old pilot was found strapped in the cockpit of his machine. The coroner attributed Brendel's accidental death to the forehead trauma; this was probably caused when the plane dived into the water.

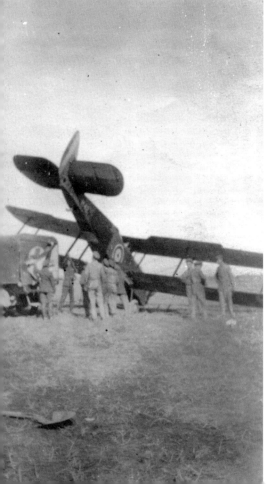

When the station closed at the end of hostilities the thirty-seven aircraft at Hooton were transferred to RAF Sealand, North Wales. The magnificent house fell into disrepair and was demolished. The historically important double hangers survived and are protected by Grade II listed buildings status.

In the air and sea increased aircraft and vessels were urgently required. On 15 September, *The Wallasey News* reported:

> 'The Ministry of Munitions is now demanding a new species of woman worker. It offers a free special training course to any woman between eighteen and thirty-five in shipbuilding and fitting. Already 32,000 students

A crashed aircraft

have qualified for work in the shipbuilding yard. They are employed on highly skilled work such as making engines, pumps and fittings and mountings for boilers. Some are engaged as oxy-acetylene operators. The recruiting centre for women shipbuilders is the Ministry of Munitions.'

The Royal Navy had a rare stroke of luck in late September, when the German mine-laying submarine *UC44* struck a mine and sank off the Waterford coast. On salvaging the vessel, the Admiralty recovered vital intelligence including how, under cover of darkness, U-boats passed over the English Channel anti-submarine nets.

The nets were transgressed by 253 submarines in ten months, this reduced journey time to the Western Approaches by eight days in comparison to the North Sea route, saved fuel, and extended by eight days the submarine's patrol. However, admiralty staff failed to deploy counter measures. Finally, on 15 December the First Sea Lord lost his patience and ordered the bolt-hole to be closed. Surface patrols were increased and the barrage was brightly illuminated at night by searchlights; the new measures immediately had a significant impact on German submarine operations.

could have sweared I saw a torpedo.

The war at sea may have shifted in favour of the Allies, but on land the troops were fighting to a standstill. The ambulance trains provided a barometer of battlefield casualties, during the first two weeks of October the energetic members of the BRCS Cheshire VAD T (Transport Section), had a busy month.

The Birkenhead News reported:

'Shortly after midnight on Friday an ambulance train arrived with 200 wounded (all sitting cases), and on Sunday another train of 218 wounded men and eight officers arrived. These brought the month's total up to 1,200 received in our local hospitals. The Saturday arrivals were distributed as: Borough Hospital 20, Hemingford Street 11, Manor Hill 12, Mersey Park 18, Bromborough 8, Ionic Street 18, Tranmere 38, Hoylake 10, Arrowe Hall 17, Temple Road 20, Wallasey Town Hall 34; total 206.

On Sunday 100 cot cases and 18 sitting up cases together with two officers (cot) and six officers (sitting up) were received. They were divided in the following manner: Fazakerley 3 officers, Croxteth Hall 5 officers, Borough Hospital 30, Bromborough 30, Temple Road 6, Ionic Street 6, Neston 4, Parkgate 6, Wallasey 10, Tranmere 106, Manor Hill 20. Total: Officers 8, Tommies 218.

On 20 October, the Hemingford Street hospital pierrot troupe posed for the camera, prior to a grand musical evening for their fellow patients and guests. The pierotts headlined the entertainment supported by fellow patients giving renditions of popular songs.

The men and women of the mercantile marine were the unsung

Once on the road to recovery, some the Hemingford Street patients participated in the then fashionable amateur dramatics or ad hoc musical acts including pierrot troupes.

Birkenhead ship yard workers are dwarfed by the war damage hole in the SS Anchored

heroes of the First World War, 14,661 perished in the service of their country and countless more survived the trauma and consequences of torpedo attacks. A portion of the mauled vessels managed to limp to friendly ports to be dry-docked for repairs, it frequently proved a grisly task as reported in a censored 20 October press article.

On 23 September, a vessel on Admiralty orders left Avonmouth, early on the morning of the 26th the vessel was torpedoed in the engine room. Three men were reported missing, but despite great damage, the crew brought the ship to port. Later, the vessel entered the West Float and berthed in a graving dock to undergo repair by Messrs Grayson's Limited.

The mutilated body of ship's engineer Patrick of Chelsea was discovered in the vessel. On 9 October, Cecil Holden, the Birkenhead coroner held an inquest during which he praised the bravery of the mercantile marine. A week later another inquest was necessary.

George May Edwards of 49, Whitford Street, Birkenhead, a chargehand boilermaker, was informed on 16 October a boot had been seen under the starboard boiler. Edwards moved a plate and then could see the leg of a man, after proceeding to remove a quantity of rubbish he brought out the body of Alfred Hale, a 23-year-old Bristol man.

The jury found the death was due to asphyxia from immersion, consequent upon the vessel having been torpedoed by a submarine.

In early November the members of the Executive Committee of the Cheshire War Agricultural Committee made their first inspection of work in progress in the neighbourhood of Bidston and Leasowe. The committee expressed satisfaction on the progress made by 140 paid German prisoners of war who were billeted at Leasowe Castle, the bed of the stream being cleared of its years of accumulations of reed, silt, etc and proper banks formed. Originally the committee intended halting the work until the spring in view of the bad weather and flooded conditions, but the work continued in readiness for spring crops.

The weather had also conspired against the British Third Ypres offensive which had failed to gain its key objectives, namely the liberation of the Belgian ports of Zeebrugge and Ostend and the capture of Roulers military railhead. Undeterred, the British launched the Battle of Cambrai, an ambitious scheme to pierce the Hindenburg Line strongpoints south-east of Arras, cross the St Quentin canal, seize the Cambrai railhead and capture Bourlon Ridge. The blows would fall on a five-mile front and involve the first en masse deployment of 476 tanks, including 'Birkenhead'.

The battle commenced on 20 November, the 'shock and awe' of tanks trundling over trenches stunned the Germans. But, the success of the first few days waned as the British were unable to maintain momentum due to a shortage of infantry reserves, mechanical failure and the vulnerability of lumbering tanks to German short-range artillery. The tank 'Birkenhead' was knocked out by a shell on the 21st, it was repaired a few days later, nine days after it was badly scarred at Gouzeaucourt. But, a series of German counter-attacks typified the Teutonic ability to redress the balance and once again neither belligerent could produce the winning card; the fighting continued into December.

Servicemen traumatised by the constant stress of mechanised warfare could develop shell-shock, the symptoms of which included panic attacks, strange behaviour, indifference to military discipline or in extreme case withdrawal into a catatonic state which might last several years. The fledgling science of psychology gradually convinced the military the condition was a mental illness not a manifestation of cowardice, the more fortunate psychiatric patients received sympathetic treatment in idyllic surroundings, but such opportunities were rare.

The Mendall Home

Mr and Mrs Edmund Johnston decided to leave the district in September; they offered their rural Bromborough home to the Red Cross, for the duration of the war and a certain time afterwards. But, the generous offer needed developing and Mr Johnston kindly made a second offer. The matter was handed over to the Mayor, who, together with his committee successfully brought the scheme to a satisfactory conclusion. The Mendell Home officially opened on 28 November, as a home for discharged sailors and soldiers, especially for those suffering from neurasthenia (chronic mental and physical fatigue and depression) and other forms of war shock. At the time of opening the home already had ten patients, this number later increased to some forty patients. It was hoped the fresh air, interest in the gardens and animals would aid the recovery of the patients. A prominent feature of the house was the Mary Barnes' Memorial Ward, £10,000 having been donated towards the running costs by Miss Barnes of Fulshaw House, Wilmslow, in memory of her sister.

As fears of a German invasion or bombing prevailed, the 1,500 strong 3/Cheshire left Bidston camp for Newcastle-on-Tyne. Twelve months later they were at West Hartlepool as part of the Tees Garrison.

On 15 December the Comrades of the Great War Cheshire Association was formed. This was one of four non-political associations representing the rights of former servicemen and women. The four associations merged on 15 May 1921 to form the British Legion; the first branch in the country was founded in Park Road East, Birkenhead and continues to help ex-service personnal.

But there was no unison in Russia which had descended into civil war and anarchy. On 16 December an armistice was signed on the Eastern Front, thus releasing German troops to prosecute the war on the Western Front. As victory hung in the balance, for the warring nations there was little goodwill and peace on earth as the fourth wartime Christmas approached, indeed the crew of the German mine-laying submarine *UC 75* carried on their duties with murderous intent laying mines off the Mersey estuary.

About 3am on 28 December the pilot boat *Alfred H. Read* of the Lighthouse and Pilotage Authorities took up station when a loud explosion occurred holing the vessel amidships in the forward part of the engine room. Those in the engine room were either killed outright by the explosion or badly injured. Most of the forty-three men onboard were in their bunks. The pilot boat sank within two minutes, bows foremost and without having heeled over to one side or other. Five men managed to grab lifebelts and jump into the Mersey and after a twenty-minute interval the small boats of another pilot boat responding to the explosion arrived and rescued three men.

The survivors, Alfred Davies (20) of Denton Drive, Liscard (apprentice), John R. Sweetman (19) of 32 Alton Road, Tuebrook (apprentice) and Edward Beckett (18) of 61, Cecil Road, West Croydon, London (Marconi Operator) were taken to hospital in Liverpool where Davies was declared dead, taking the death toll to forty-one. Inexplicably the censor concealed the loss of the vessel until later when questions asked in the House of Commons revealed the fate of the *Alfred H. Read*.

CHAPTER 6

1918 - The Final Blows

In contrast to the work of the censor, Government propaganda lauded the increasing number of American troop ships arriving in French and British ports. Expectations were high that the great untapped human reservoir of keen but inexperienced American Expeditionary Force would restore numerical superiority before Germany could fully complete the transfer of troops from east to west battlefronts. But Germany was one step ahead, a wealth of preordained plans had been gathering dust in German headquarters for some time; one such plan, code named Operation Michael, was adapted for a Spring offensive. In the meantime British strategy changed from offensive to defensive, confidently believing they could repulse any attempted German breakthrough. The distant Royal Navy blockade continued to exert an ever-tightening stranglehold on German imports, leading to civil unrest among the malnourished civilian population.

Against this backdrop, the mendacious Lloyd George, with one eye on home front productivity and the other on servicemen casualties, had, for some time, been restricting the flow of men to France. During February British infantry divisions on the Western Front were reduced from a twelve-battalion basis to nine battalion-strong units. Included in the disbanded battalions were the locally raised 16/Cheshire and 13/Cheshire; despite the protestations of prominent local dignitaries the Wirral battalion passed into history.

In spite of the voluntary reduction in food consumption mandatory food rationing was introduced locally on 4 February. Households were required to register and to assist in the process, local schools aided people to complete the paperwork. In Wallasey alone, 22,600 application forms had to be dealt with and about 91,000 ration cards had to be filled in. Retailers could only serve customers registered with their business. The four mandatory categories in the ration books being Sugar retailer – Fats retailer – Butcher – Bacon, but these, if available, could generally be purchased during a single visit to the local grocer. The national meat scheme came into operation on 7 April.

The food shortages were yet another problem for women, now accustomed to the absence of their military husbands. They often juggled their housekeeping chores with munitions work. Within this category was Charlotte Evelyn Massey of 28 Percy Road, Seacombe. Her husband was serving in France when Charlotte became a munitions worker in the employ of Messrs Rowlands of Seacombe. She had worked on a particular shell-drilling machine for a week and turned out fifty to sixty shells a day. On 6 February, contrary to regulations, the 28-year-old fitted a shell into her machine while it was in motion. She became caught in the machine and her body was wrapped around the machine two or three times. Mrs Massey died the next day in Victoria Central Hospital. A post mortem determined an accidental death resulting from the shock from the injuries and heart failure. Mrs Massey had unwittingly given her life in the cause of freedom and provided the insatiable war with one more victim.

WALLASEY FOOD CONTROL COMMITTEE.

TO ALL HOUSEHOLDERS:

TO-DAY (SATURDAY),

IS THE

LAST DAY for REGISTRATION

WITH RETAILERS FOR FOOD SUPPLIES.

The following articles will be rationed as from MONDAY NEXT, February 4th, 1918.

Sugar	....	....	....	**Half pound** each person.
Tea	....	....	....	**1½ ounces** each person.
Butter or Margarine	....			**Four ounces** each person
Meat	....	....	....	**One pound** each person.

There will be no need to crush at the shops. Every person will get their fair share of what the Retailer is able to provide.

If stocks are too little to give the full ration, every householder will be reduced to equal quantities, no matter which day in the week they do their shopping.

In no case will more than the rationed portions be served.

Retailers can only serve Registered Customers.

BY ORDER.

Wallasey Food Control Committee.

In fiscal terms, the daily cost of the war to Britain was £6,384,000 prompting King George to state: 'I am confident my people are willing to contribute, both now, and in the future, whatever money may be necessary to secure victory.'

The Chancellor of the Exchequer, Andrew Bonar Law adopted a different tack.

'I should like those at the head of great financial institutions to convert to whatever extent they can Treasury Bills and take out War Bonds instead. The second thing I want the people of this country to do is save every penny they can of expenditure and lend their savings to the state.'

The country was asked to raise £100,000,000 in War Bonds and War Savings and every town of considerable size was set the task of providing the money for some weapon of war – a Dreadnought battleship, a battle cruiser, a destroyer or an aeroplane. Wallasey chose to finance a naval monitor vessel; Liverpool easily raised funds for a Dreadnought and Birkenhead opted to raise £400,000 for a battle cruiser.

ILLUMINATED TANK.

TO-DAY, WEDNESDAY, MAR. 6th, 7.50, New Ferry Terminus. Principal Speaker— HON. W. HULME LEVER.	INVEST IN THE TRAM CAR BANK TOWARDS BIRKENHEAD'S CRUISER.	Friday, March 8th, 7 o'clock, MARKET PLACE SOUTH. Saturday, March 9th, 7 o'clock, CHARING CROSS. BAND IN ATTENDANCE.

Open-air Display of War Pictures, including the " Sinking of the Lusitania " Grange-road EVERY EVENING. Birkenhead War savings Committee.

Of an evening Birkenhead temporarily used two tramcars to promote war saving. One was illuminated in red, white and blue lights and placarded with war savings appeals and pictures. The other was an imitation tank adapted from the repair tramcar. 'The body was covered with laths and cardboard, all painted a drab colour, on a design which gave a capital imitation of an actual tank, for there were loopholes with dummy guns peeping out. Hundreds of red, white and blue electric

Have **YOU** helped your Country?

Thousands of our bravest and best are willing to GIVE their lives for Britain. Is it too much to ask you to LEND your money to help them in their fight for freedom?

YOU CAN BUY WAR BONDS.

lights outline and otherwise illuminate the tank; the sides bear war savings placards and pictures of a battle cruiser.'

The War Bonds proved very successful and were emulated in the Second World War. The actual Birkenhead investments up to Monday evening were most encouraging, and about midday on Tuesday the figures were posted up conspicuously outside the town hall under the truism 'Money means victory'. The total shown was £181,551 made up as follows: Alfred Holt & Co £100,000; Birkenhead Corporation £35,000; Bonds through banks £42,945; Certificates through banks £3,606. By Saturday, 9 March the fund had reached half a million pounds, more than enough for a cruiser. Wallasey struggled to raise monitor funding as the residents had contributed to the Liverpool and Birkenhead schemes.

As the citizens focused on 'If you can't fight, invest all you can', others introduced arrangements for protection from daytime air raids, owing to the extended range of aircraft. The warning came into operation on 15 March. On the approach of hostile aircraft two maroons would be fired at twenty second intervals and detonate with a loud explosion at approximately 900 feet, alerting the public to take cover. It's assumed the Birkenhead and Liscard anti-aircraft batteries would then have engaged the aircraft.

The warnings operated between half an hour before sunrise and a half hour after sunset. When danger passed, the public were informed by police on bicycles blowing their whistles and carrying cards bearing 'All Clear'. The night time alert system of reducing electric lighting gradually for ten minutes and then shutting it off completely and the reduction of gas lighting remained operative for twenty-four hours.

Four days later, 30-year-old Gertrude Mary Martin of Mount House, Prenton died. She was a member of Cheshire 126 VAD for which she worked so strenuously her health broke down. The funeral took place at Flaybrick cemetery, where at the cemetery gate the cortege was met by a large contingent from Ionic Street, Rock Ferry and Abbotsford hospitals and marched in procession to the chapel. The Reverend J.E. Woodward read an impressive address touching on the fact Miss Martin had laid down her life for king and country as sure as any soldier.

Meanwhile General Ludendorff finalised plans for a major offensive between St Quentin on the Somme and the Arras sector, a battle front of almost fifty miles. The main blows would fall on the Anglo-French army boundary and inevitably create maximum confusion. After breaching the Allied line, German troops would then head north and sweep the under-strength British force into the sea. A decisive victory would have produced a similar result to the 1940 Fall of France. Douglas Haig reported sixty-four German divisions were amassed against twenty-nine infantry British divisions and three cavalry divisions, of which nineteen were in the line.

On 21 March the German spring offensive began, this comprised four codenamed phases, the initial and most powerful being Operation Michael aimed at defeating the British on the Somme compelling the French to seek an armistice. Operations Georgette, Gneisenau and Blucher-Yorck were designed to divert Allied forces from the Somme and reduce resistance. The static war suddenly became a war of mobility; weakened Allied positions were over-run, the Fifth Army withdrew, in the process abandoning the Somme battlefields, but focusing their resources on the route to the Channel ports and the railhead at Amiens. Stiffening resistance and the rapid pace of the German advance prevented the replenishment of supplies and ammunition, the momentum of the advance was lost and the Allied crisis briefly abated. The British had suffered 178,000 casualties, the French 92,000 but the Germans incurred 239,000 casualties, yet the fighting soon continued with renewed vigour in a desperate attempt to grasp the laurels of victory before American intervention.

But evidence of British resilience was about to be driven home with a vengeance. The Wallasey Corporation Ferries *Iris* and *Daffodil* were powerful and easily manoeuvrable and each had capacity for 1,600 passengers. Both ferries were requisitioned by the Admiralty and on 23 April played a key role in a combined naval and Royal Marine amphibious assault against the fortified Zeebrugge harbour wall known as the Mole. During the height of the land assault, three block ships, *Thetis, Intrepid* and *Iphigenia* slipped into the shell-swept Zeebrugge harbour and scuttled themselves across the channel to prevent U-boats from leaving the harbour. The gallantry displayed throughout the combined operation was recognised by the award of eight Victoria Crosses.

The block ship operation proved unsuccessful for during high tide U-boats and destroyers were able to bypass the block ships, but nonetheless it was a great feat of arms. The raids humiliated the German fleet and implanted the grain of doubt that led to mutinies at Kiel, a precursor to the surrender of the German Navy.

The Admiralty played their morale boosting trump card for all it was worth. The patched-up ferries were made available for public inspection at Falmouth, admission by voluntary donation, and Portsmouth where 12,000 visitors paid 6d (2.5p). The fees were donated to appropriate naval charities.

On Friday, 17 May, the shell-battered vessels returned to the Mersey and were accorded a warm reception. Then next day the Wallasey Mayor, corporation officials and Liverpool guests boarded the vessels for a river trip. Later in the day the boats were taken into Canning

Daffodil's triumphant return to the Mersey.

The shell battered Iris.

Dock, Liverpool where they went on public display from Sunday until Tuesday evening. The admittance price was a shilling per visitor. Over the weekend 10,000 visitors toured the boats; a reduced admission on Bank Holiday Monday produced another influx. The proceeds, including souvenir programmes and picture postcards of the scarred ferries, totalled £1,380. Of this, £500 provided an *Iris* and *Daffodil* bed at the local hospital; the balance went to naval charities and the Red Cross. Weeks later, in recognition of their gallantry, George V granted both ferries the prefix Royal, a distinction proudly borne by the current *Royal Iris* and *Royal Daffodil*.

THE FLOWERS OF THE FLEET

They are here with scars of battle,
Iris *and the* Daffodil,
Ready once again for action.
Waiting on the people's will;

Gather in your crowds to view them,
Helping on the cause of right,
By your gifts to wounded heroes
From the gory Zeebrugge fight.

Look ye on those battered warriors,
That so boldly faced the Hun,
Then decide we must not falter
Till the victory is won;

Ye may gain a place of honour,
By your acts of self-denial;
Standing bravely by your country
In her agony and trial.

Flordelisa

The Zeebrugge and Ostend raids uplifted the nation's self confidence during a period of crisis, the media coverage overshadowed briefly lesser events including a dramatic anti-hero local incident on the afternoon of 2 May.

Mr Bead of Leasowe Farm, together with a friend from Wallasey, went out in a sailing boat. The sea was choppy and the boat was overturned. One of the men attempted to reach the shore for help while the other clung to the boat. Sergeant J. Phillips, Welsh Regiment and Private B. Mathews, Royal Defence Corps, both plunged into the sea to assist the first man who had got into difficulties and was drowning. They succeeded in reaching the embankment in an exhausted condition. The guard in charge of the German prisoners of war was appealed to by a German prisoner named Bunte, to be allowed to rescue the man clinging to the upturned boat. He was a fine swimmer and brought the exhausted man ashore amid the cheers of the crowd.

When wounded soldiers were recuperating at Leasowe Castle they had the use of a loaned billiard board, but the lender objected to its use by the German prisoners and demanded its return. Days before Christmas the prisoners returned the board to its owner's house, where a prisoner noticed a photograph of one of the Olympic teams. On it was his own photograph, he was an international swimmer, could this have been Bunte?

The Germans occupied large French industrial areas including coalfields. In an age when 'coal was king' Britain exported her own precious coal for use in French industry and warships. A shortage of miners and high demand for coal led to the government introducing coal restrictions. On Sunday, 5 May, the Mersey Electric Railway was compelled to reduce its fuel consumption by fifteen per cent. Train services were reduced during day-time, but the heavy evening business service between 1700 and 1900 hours remained unaffected. Services began later and finished earlier, even so, the last train from Liverpool to Park Station departed at 2307 hours. The tram cars also finished thirty minutes earlier, more stringent cuts were avoided due to the travel needs of munition workers.

Armament works were now routinely checked for men carrying out work that could be done by women. The quest for men expanded its parameters in April when the Military Service Act extended

compulsory military service to 51-year-olds. In May, regardless of their occupation any men born 1898-99 were called up. The military dispensation for male war production workers was reviewed, by mid 1918 this policy yielded a further 100,000 conscripts.

At Port Sunlight village, on the insistence of the now Lord Leverhulme, a war memorial committee was formed in April 1916, and

the eminent sculptor, Sir W. Goscombe John was invited to submit a design, which was approved on 26 June the same year. The design featured a cross with bronze figures at the base, the figures in heroic size (7ft 6ins or 2.3m) representing a soldier defending women and children and a fallen comrade by his side. At the base of the cross would be inscribed the names of those who had given their life in the war. The design included bas-reliefs representing the navy and air force and sculpture groups of children, there being a total of eight groups. The memorial would cost an estimated £10,000.

In mid May, a well attended meeting at the Lyceum, Port Sunlight met to further progress the scheme. The Hon W. Hulme Lever presided and amongst those on the platform was Lord Leverhulme. During the course of the meeting it was accepted that 'no memorial could do full justice to the sacrifice of the fallen, but it would commemorate their deeds and tell to future generations of the manner in which the men went forth to risk their lives.' Lord Leverhulme also stated: 'The question of a war memorial raised many points including the suggestion of what he termed a utility war memorial. What they wanted to put up at Port Sunlight was a memorial which for all time would be their pride, joy and pleasure.' In this Port Sunlight succeeded; today the memorial is regarded as one of the nation's finest war memorials.

At the beginning of May, the Scala Cinema, Seacombe presented one of the most popular comical plays of the Great War, *The Better 'Ole*, by Captain Bruce Bairnsfather and Captain Arthur Eliot. Readers may be familiar with the wonderful character of Old Bill from postcards, books and chinaware. Audiences laughed at Old Bill, although many felt a lump in their throat when they witnessed him risking his life to save the

The Better 'Ole

division, or soliloquising in his few spare moments upon those who were waiting for him.

As were the family of missing soldier Private John McGreal of the 3/Connaught Rangers, who resided at 32 Bray Street, Birkenhead. The 22-year-old returned home from Newcastle on 6 April for seven days leave. Feeling unwell he visited the doctor who advised he was consumptive (had TB), other visits to a doctor followed and resulted in two extensions of leave. On 27 April, he went for a walk and did not return, the police were informed. On 19 May, two policemen recovered a khaki-clad soldier's body from the West Float; papers on him confirmed it was the missing soldier. His father confirmed identification and said the deceased seemed in very high spirits on the day in question. He had never threatened to commit suicide.

A doctor advised that although the body was decomposed, it was apparent deceased had entered the water alive. The coroner concluded, from the evidence that the deceased might have got into the water accidentally. Private John McGreal is buried in a communal military grave within Flaybrick cemetery.

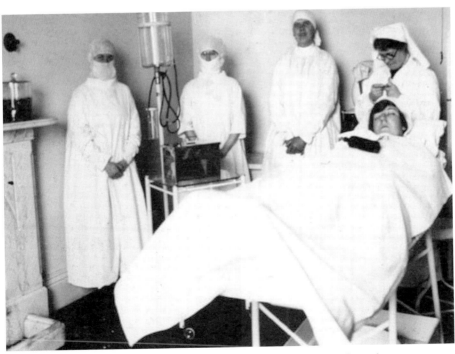

Given the period's limitations in surgery and medicine we can only conjecture how many lives could have been saved, if today's advances in medicine were available. Certainly the posed 5 May 1918 photograph of the operating theatre at Manor Hill hospital does little to inspire confidence in surgical procedures or equipment, not forgetting the bacteria-laden fireplace.

The army was losing hundreds of men a day and replacing them was becoming increasingly difficult. Sir Aukland Geddes, director of National Service circulated a letter to local authorities increasing pressure on military tribunals to produce more recruits:

'At the present critical stage of the war even greater efforts and sacrifices than those already made are necessary on the part of all classes of the community. The demand for men in the higher medical grades or categories is insistent, and must be met at once if the national forces are to be maintained in adequate strength. No fit man of fighting age should now receive exemption on occupation grounds unless he is engaged on work directly important to the prosecution of the war. There is a general paramount necessity that an increased flow of fit men should be obtained without delay to furnish his Majesty's Forces the support which is essential.'

Amongst those not wearing khaki were the Great Western Railway staff and shipyard workers of Cheshire 19A and 19B VAD, formed in August 1914. By mid June 1918 they had dealt with 114 ambulance trains conveying 21,126 wounded to Birkenhead and district. A correspondent writing on the duties undertaken said:

The Walter Harding ambulance was presented to the Red Cross 12 April 1916

'Upon the arrival of an ambulance train these men parade at their head quarters and from there may be sent to any hospital as orderlies to carry the patients from the ambulances to different wards. No man leaves the hospital until every patient has been washed or bathed and is comfortable in bed. They may on the other hand, be drafted to the station to act as stretcher bearers from the train to the ambulances. When a train arrives at Woodside it is handed over to these detachments for unloading. The last train of 340 sitting cases was cleared in eighteen minutes. The Commandant has had several compliments on the expeditious manner in which the unloading has been carried out.'

In a series of bitterly contested engagements the Allies reversed German fortunes on the Western Front. On 15 July, near Reims, Ludendorff launched his final great offensive but made little progress. Three days later a Franco-American counter-attack supported by masses of light tanks drove back the Germans. Depleted of reserves and weakened by 50,000 casualties, on 20 July Ludendorff abandoned his Flanders offensive and went on the offensive.

Thousands of German prisoners were held in the United Kingdom. Those held locally were hired out by the Cheshire Agricultural Committee at the same average rates of pay as local agricultural workers. The average day was eight and a half hours and double time was paid for overtime.

At Wallasey Borough Police Court on Monday 1 August two Wallasey domestic servants B. McHugh (35) a cook, and Lily Fleet (24) a nurse, appeared on remand to answer charges of transmitting to a prisoner of war, cigarettes, tobacco and flowers which was likely to interfere with the discipline of a place of detention, without the necessary authority and therefore committing an offence prohibited by the DORA regulations 7 June 1918.

Both ladies were employed at a house in Groveland Avenue and German prisoners from Leasowe Castle were engaged nearby removing sand. The defendants were frequently seen loitering near a specially-erected German prisoner's toilet. A suspicious guard noticed disturbed sand in the toilet, a search discovered a brown parcel containing tobacco and cigarettes and a letter addressed to a German prisoner signed by Fleet. The sentry saw a U-boat commander enter the toilet and search the sand.

On 16 July, the police searched the defendant's former place of employment and discovered numerous letters from the prisoners of war, also photographs of German prisoners. The German prisoners had been searched and letters written by the defendants were found in their possession, these had not passed through the censor.

The accused were sentenced for three months on each charge, the term to run concurrently, they were sternly informed 'they showed an entire lack of loyalty'.

By now there was an abundance of American Army troops on Merseyside, consequently about 22 June, the Mayors of Liverpool, Birkenhead, Bootle and Wallasey attended a conference in Liverpool Town Hall with regard to offering hospitality and entertainment to them.

The scheme for organising home hospitality for American soldiers throughout the nation was proposed and initiated by the Liverpool branch of the Rotary Club. Merseyside was divided into twenty districts; eight of these were in the Wirral peninsula. Under the scheme, wounded soldiers, on the last week of their convalescence from hospital which was the only opportunity Army regulations allowed, were entertained as honoured guests in private homes. There they would…

The staff and some wounded pose for the camera outside Wallasey Town Hall military hospital.

'learn at first hand the nature of our home life, so that in writing home, and when they return home as living epistles, they may clear the air of the poison mists, which are enemies, with their usual thoroughness, are spreading over there in the hope of weakening the alliance which we believe is to prove fatal to their hopes.'

The scheme was evidently a great success as during the twelve months of its existence, four different commanding officers of Mossley Hill American Red Cross Hospital wrote favourable letters of appreciation.

Over one and a quarter million American Expeditionary Force men were now in France and, although inexperienced, their presence had a demoralising effect on German forces' morale. Allied counter-attacks were many, but the most significant of the final blows occurred near Amiens on 8 August. The surprise Anglo-French attack broke against a demoralised enemy increasingly fighting without conviction. General Ludendorff later described 8 August as 'the black day of the German Army in the history of the war... it put the decline of our fighting power beyond all doubt'. The Allied advance to victory had begun.

The German tide began to ebb and gradually withdrew in the direction of the Fatherland. Ludendorff admitted the war could not be won, but wished to maintain a strong military position to negotiate favourable terms in the inevitable peace treaty, ideally retaining possession of Belgium and Luxemburg. Austria promised to send reinforcements to France, but a few weeks later attempted to broker a peace deal with the United States; it was declined. On 27 September Bulgaria also sought an armistice, followed by the abdication of their monarch.

In early September, questions in the Commons over German prisoners' continued use of the Railwaymen's Convalescent Home at Leasowe Castle reflected a local ground swell of opinion against the German prisoners who were considered to be residing in far superior accommodation than the 17/South Lancashire (Transport Workers) battalion based at Bidston. This, combined with the request of the National Union of Railwaymen, led to the authorities rebuilding the partially dismantled Bidston camp (some huts had been removed for American troops) and contrary to the objections of the village residents, it became a prison camp. The military and railwaymen appear to have shared the castle.

During the final advance to victory Second Lieutenant Smallwood of Rosemount, Oxton, Birkenhead was the tank commander of *Birkenhead*, he was awarded the Military Cross for gallantry near Holnon on 18 September 1918. When the infantry were unable to advance owing to very heavy machine-gun fire he cleverly steered *Birkenhead* through smoke, darkness and heavy rain to his objective over 3,000 yards away. Though subjected to intense close range fire he kept all his guns going. *Birkenhead* became ditched when crossing a sunken road. In spite of gallant efforts on the part of himself and his first driver it could not be extricated. Another tank caught fire, all the crew were captured except the tank commander whom Smallwood rescued. During this time the infantry were 300 yards behind and unable to advance. Smallwood kept the enemy at bay with *Birkenhead's* machine-guns, meanwhile sending a message to the infantry advising the situation was in hand and to advance.

Late September witnessed the defeat of the Turkish armies in Palestine. Faced with the collapse of the alliance between the Central Powers, Germany became increasingly isolated prompting Ludendorff to demand an armistice, to which the Kaiser agreed. On 5 November the Admiralty announced they had successfully defeated the submarines and maintained a huge convoy system. Of the 85,772 merchant ships convoyed only 433 were lost. Germany's key allies Turkey and Austria-Hungary signed armistices on 30 November and 3 November respectively. Her own peace negotiations stalled over President Wilson's insistence on the abdication of Kaiser Wilhelm II.

Exasperated by the Kaiser's reluctance, the German Chancellor forced the Kaiser's hand by announcing his abdication on 9 November (he officially abdicated on 28 November). Two days later Germany signed an armistice signifying a ceasefire. The Great War for civilisation was over.

The 16th November edition of *The Wallasey News* reported how the good news was received in Wallasey:

'People went to their business as usual on Monday. Conscious of the fact that the last shot would soon be fired they were determined to work to the last minute. The [flour] mills and the munitions factories and the shipyards carried on with the knowledge that the end was near.

'Yet the change came with dramatic suddenness, and the ordered life of the workshop gave place to pandemonium. About 10.30am official news came across the wire to the newspaper offices at Seacombe, and no sooner was it published on hastily printed posters than the streets were bedecked with flags. Soon afterwards the news spread to the broad Mersey and dockyards, and a burst of noise arose that put "Mafficking" [relief of Mafeking] days in the shade. Steam pipes and whistles shrieked discordantly, bells were rung and ferry boats fussed about rivalling each other in their uproar. The deep-throated sirens of the liners and the shrill whistle of the tug boats took up the message and carried it for miles inland. At the various large workshops men and women "downed tools" immediately, and the streets, which a few minutes before were almost deserted, were now well-nigh impassable.

I WON'T HAVE PEACE UNTIL I HEAR FROM YOU!

'Local shopkeepers must have anticipated the demand for flags, for nearly everyone carried small editions of the Union Jack, which they brandished with joy, and at the same time imparted the information that it was "the stuff to give 'em".. Munition and mill girls marched arm-in-arm through the streets singing patriotic songs and bestowing their favours at times most lavishly on soldier friends and male acquaintances, some of them seemed glad to get the ordeal over. It was a good-natured happy crowd. The suspense of years had suddenly snapped, and the *dreadful war which had brought so much sorrow to so many of them was at last over. Surely there was never such a time of gladness, and the cheering multitudes were determined that "the day" should live long in the minds of themselves and their children. Maroons added their compliment to the din, and railway signals banged their accompaniments.*

'Towards night the excitement increased, and processions singing popular songs marched through the main streets, while in the open spaces of the town huge bonfires brilliantly illuminated the surroundings and provided endless delight to the younger generation, although even the older ones let themselves go on this occasion, and danced around the flames when the Kaiser's effigy was hurled to destruction. Every good day, however has its end, and the crowds, tired out with shouting and perambulating, at last dispersed to their homes. There was little excess, for drink was almost unobtainable, most of the local houses being on short supplies, and although there was an essential shortage of spirits it was astonishing how many people had put a bottle by for "the end of the war". And they certainly could not welcome a better day for England. They did so soberly, and with the relief of a peril passed.'

Warfare on the Western Front had ceased but elsewhere the war continued. A military machine and supporting infrastructure assembled in excess of four years would take time to dismantle before life returned to normal and families and communities recovered from apocalyptic warfare. Men optimistically posted as missing were presumed dead but with no identified remains families usually waited in vain for glad tidings concerning their loved one.

Despite the ending of hostilities the American

" Lest we Forget."	
Killed - -	686,623
Wounded - -	2,049,199
Presumed Dead -	97,000
Unaccounted for	64,800
Total - -	2,897,622

'Thanksgiving Day,' was not overlooked on Merseyside, the invitations were issued to 1,000 American sailors and about 1,000 ladies were invited to meet them. The entertainment was provided for in Birkenhead Town Hall, Bootle Town Hall and Birkenhead Town Hall.

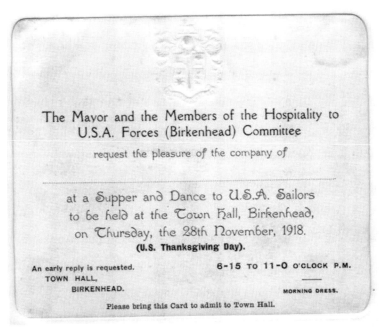

The Mayor and the Members of the Hospitality to U.S.A. Forces (Birkenhead) Committee

request the pleasure of the company of

at a Supper and Dance to U.S.A. Sailors to be held at the Town Hall, Birkenhead, on Thursday, the 28th November, 1918.

(U.S. Thanksgiving Day).

An early reply is requested.　　　　6-15 TO 11-0 O'CLOCK P.M.
TOWN HALL,
　　BIRKENHEAD.
　　　　　　　　　　　　　　MORNING DRESS.

Please bring this Card to admit to Town Hall.

The military began to demobilise, priority being given to miners and other occupations so desperately needed at home. This caused great resentment to men who had signed up for a period designated 'duration of war only' and for most it would be early spring before they returned home. The wounded still needed tending, there would be no remarkable peacetime recovery, and indeed legions would die for decades from Great War injuries.

Christmas in the local military hospitals was as festive as ever. *The Wallasey News* in a rare reference to Wallasey's largest military hospital commented:

'The wards were very tastefully decorated and the patients regaled with seasonal fare through the generous help afforded the committee who have so long undertaken the good work of providing extra comforts for the wounded. While the Christmas

dinner was in progress the hospital was visited by the Mayor (Councillor W. Eastwood), and the Mayoress (Mrs E.H. Humphreys). In the evening there was a fancy dress carnival followed by a whist drive.'

The treatment of patients tapered off during 1919, but the building was not available for municipal purposes until 3 November 1920.

The Treaty of Versailles, symbolically signed on the fifth anniversary

The 1918 New Year's Carnival at Wallasey Town Hall military hospital

of the outbreak of war formally ended the European war. This made little difference to units including the 17/Kings Liverpool who were engaged in Northern Russia against the Bolsheviks. It would be early September 1919 before the last of the battalion boarded the troopship for home. Sadly, the uncompromising and humiliating terms of surrender reluctantly accepted by a vanquished Germany produced a festering resentment; two decades later the world would again be at war. In the post war years towns and cities erected war memorials.

Hamilton Square Cenotaph, Birkenhead designed by Liverpool architect Lionel Budden and created by Herbert Tyson Smith was unveiled on 5 July 1925 by General Sir Richard H.K. Butler. Budden and Tyson Smith later produced the Liverpool cenotaph.

Wallasey War Memorial sculpted by Bernie Rhind of Edinburgh, stands on Magazine Promenade. The memorial was unveiled by Lord Derby on 26 January 1921.

The Hoylake and West Kirby war memorial.

The Hoylake and West Kirby war memorial on the summit of Grange Hill was officially unveiled in mid December 1922. The 40-foot high obelisk of Cornish granite has two bronze figures sculptured by Charles Sergeant Jagger. A soldier with his back to the wall, so to speak, symbolises the defence of liberty and freedom. On the west side is a figure of humanity, standing on a globe supported by three crosses. During the mid-December 1922 unveiling, Earl Birkenhead referred to the six gallant Johnstone sons commemorated, five died, accounts vary about the survivor who either had both legs shot off or his feet sliced off when he slipped boarding a troop train.

Port Sunlight War Memorial was unveiled on 3 December 1921 by blinded ex-sergeant George Eames, who was elected by ballot. He was guided by ex-private Robert E. Cruikshank VC of Lever Brothers' London office. The company magazine *Progress* reported:

Port Sunlight War Memorial

'So it came about that the choice fell upon an old servant of the company that he should also have been the one man in that vast concourse for whom the beauty of the memorial must always be a matter of report, was a circumstance that gave the occasion added poignancy. The sightless figure of George Eames stood as the blind cruelty of war and the symbol of the dauntless soul of man triumphing over tribulation.'

George Eames, The Soldier baritone. Totally blinded on the Somme, July 1916

WARSHIPS

Built at Birkenhead during the Great War.

NAME. H.M.S.	CLASS.	DISPLACEMENT. TONS.	H.P.
BIRKENHEAD	Cruiser	6,000	27,000
CHESTER	,,	6,400	32,000
CAROLINE	Light Cruiser	3,750	40,000
CASTOR	,,	3,750	40,000
CONSTANCE	,,	3,750	40,000
CALEDON	,,	4,120	48,000
CAIRO	,,	4,190	48,000
CAPETOWN	,,	4,190	48,000
CLEOPATRA—Machinery for			40,000
CAMBRIAN—Machinery for			40,000
KEMPENFELT	Flotilla Leader	1,990	40,000
ARDIEL	,,	1,990	40,000
GABRIEL	,,	1,990	40,000
ITHURIEL	,,	1,990	40,000
PARKER	,,	1,990	40,000
GRENVILLE	,,	1,990	40,000
HOSTE	,,	1,990	40,000
SEYMOUR	,,	1,990	40,000
SAUMAREZ	,,	1,990	40,000

NAME. H.M.S.	CLASS.	DISPLACEMENT. TONS.	H.P.
VALENTINE	Flotilla Leader	1,620	40,000
VALHALLA	,,	1,620	31,000
BRUCE	,,	2,150	44,000
DOUGLAS	,,	2,150	44,000
CAMPBELL	,,	2,150	44,000
MACKAY	,,	2,150	44,000
MALCOLM	,,	2,150	44,000
E 41	Submarine	810	1,750
E 42	,,	810	1,750
E 45	,,	810	1,750
E 46	,,	810	1,750
L 7	,,	1,020	2,400
L 8	,,	1,020	2,400
R 11	,,	—	—
R 11	,,	—	—
R 12	,,	—	—
H 33	,,	—	—
H 34	,,	—	—

53

Cammell Laird
built warships
1914 - 1918

Selected bibliography and further reading

Almost an Island, the story of Wallasey. Noël E Smith. Wallasey.

The History of the Cheshire Regiment. Colonel Arthur Crookenden. Naval & Military Press Ltd.

Hooton Park, A thousand years of history. Peter Richardson. Hooton Airword. 1993.

Men of Iron, Cammell Laird Shipbuilders. D. Hollet. Countyvise Ltd, Birkenhead 1992.

Peace Pledge Union Project, an online Great War conscription resource.

The Port of Liverpool, A History. The Mersey Docks and Harbour Company.

The Rise and Progress of Wallasey. E.C. Woods and P.C. Brown. Public Libraries Department, Wallasey Corporation 1960.

Victory Souvenir of the Great War. Wilmer Brothers, Birkenhead. Circa 1920.

World War 1 Day by Day. Ian Westwell. Grange Books, Hoo, Kent, 2002.

The World War One Source Book. Philip Haythornthwaite. Arms and Armour Press, London. 1998.

Newspapers and Periodicals

Birkenhead and Cheshire Advertiser and Wallasey Guardian.

Birkenhead News. The Times. Wallasey News and Wirral General Advertiser.

Index